Hunting Moments of Truth

Hunting Moments of Truth

Edited by
Eric Peper
Jim Rikhoff

Drawings by Milton C. Weiler

WINCHESTER PRESS

Library of Congress Catalog Card Number 73–78821
ISBN: 0–87691–117–3 (regular edition)
ISBN: 0–87691–123–8 (limited edition)

Published by Winchester Press
460 Park Avenue, New York 10022

Printed in the United States of America

To
Larry Koller
Jack Randolph
John Alden Knight
Richard Alden Knight
Ralf "Pappy" Coykendall, Sr.
and
Pete Kuhlhoff

whose superb sportsmanship, fine humor
and splendid talents are missed by many of the hunters
in this book.

Contents

Grouse Gunner's Prayer

DANA S. LAMB

Give me a woodlot and an orchard by a long-abandoned barn; a cattle pasture where thorn apples grow; an old rail fence along the bank above a bog that feeds a sparkling little alder-bordered stream wherein the brook trout soon will spawn and, when the flight from farther north is on, the woodcock chalks abound. Give me the long gray grass that crowns a gentle knoll that slopes down to the sun-baked hardhack and a stand of small white birch. Give me the remnants of a briar-guarded wall, a carpet of the forest's fallen leaves beyond its mossy heaps of stones; faint traces of a one-time wagon track between the trunks of ancient oaks; a grove of evergreens, the rhododendron thick along its edge.

Give me a frosty morning on the gold and crimson hills; time-tested friends with whom I long have shared the secrets of the woods: the places where the partridge feed; which way the birds are apt to fly. Give me a snow-white setter, steady, sound and slow, who never ranges, like a quail dog, far ahead and always marks a grounded grouse; an easy-handling twenty-gauge that fits my shoulder and my arm; the strength to climb the ridges and to work the swamps and swales.

Never let me fail to gauge the distance and the speed of flying birds, to shoot straight at the target and with skill—or else to cleanly miss and not to maim. Don't let me fail to give the man who hunts beside me his

viii

full share of shots, and credit for a grouse he claims that I at first had thought had fallen to my gun. No matter how far off I am from home or whether I am coming back, don't let me fail to thank the farmer who has let me hunt behind his house.

Give me kind thoughts about the country boy who may, with rabbit hound and twenty-two, have spoiled my cover for that lovely autumn day; about a gunning partner's over-eager Brittany who puts 'em up a hundred yards ahead—I know the owner of the ill-trained dog regrets the ruin of the hunt far more than I.

Give me the eyes to see and ears to hear; to see the work of glaciers many thousand years ago in spreading boulders bigger than a woodshed or a poultry pen beneath the pines where, in this eon's later age, the bears and bobcats den; to watch, high overhead against the blue, the miracle of bird

migrations toward the south; to see, while sitting silent on a drumming log, the deer go down the hill in single file; to briefly glimpse a hunting fox; to hear the music of a distant waterfall, the chorus of a flight of crows, the chatter of a squirrel not yet gone to ground, the echoes of a shot—far off.

This is my prayer—or some of it. But who has need to pray in words? Awareness of man's dreams and knowledge of his needs exists. Today kind Providence has granted every wish a man could have. My dog lies at my feet as I await my friends. I take my brace of biddies from the pocket of my shooting coat and kneel to drink the water of an ice-cold spring.

I kneel and stay there on my knees awhile to thank my God—whatever God may be—and yours.

Foreword

Ever since man's first expedition in search of food, hunting has had its moments of truth. The hunter's moment of truth has always been a peculiarly personal instant, whether it is the silent stalk to approach the quarry; the nervous wait, hoping that the wind does not shift while the hunters drive the game to the trap; or the sickening click of a misfire after a stalk to within mere yards of a big bull elk.

For a particular hunter the moment may occur at any time. For one man it may be that always cold, yet always magic, first minute of daylight—in a duck blind, on a deer stand or under an oak while waiting for squirrels. For another it may be the few seconds it takes to drop the first shells into the gun and snap the action shut. Curiously, or perhaps not so curiously to the veteran, it is seldom the moment of the kill. It can be the instant just before the trigger is pulled, or it can be something that happened long before the game appeared. Occasionally, the most meaningful "moment" in a hunter's life may stretch over hours or even days. No matter when the moment occurs, however, it is distinguished by its purely personal nature.

The cast assembled in the pages that follow is a truly remarkable one. Each of the contributors has spent uncounted hours in the game fields—and each of them, asked to recall and assess *the* moment of truth that was most meaningful to him, had a wealth of memories to consider. Thus we have here the most dramatic or most challenging or most poignant moments of some of the best, most experienced hunters in the world.

Yet the nature of the experiences described in the following pages varies greatly from man to man. To be sure, there are a number of stories that assume the drama one would expect in a volume titled *Hunting Moments of Truth*—the charge of a rogue Cape buffalo, the exhilaration of one's first ram. There are others, however, that are very different—less dramatic on the surface, yet just as meaningful to their protagonists. And this, after all, is as it should be. This book, in a more or less circuitous fashion, answers the all too frequently asked question "Why do men hunt?"

The great exhilaration and anticipation that the hunter feels each time he goes afield is part of each story. While these are the contributors' personal "moments," by sharing them with us they allow all of us to identify with their instants and borrow a bit of their excitement.

Perhaps it may be difficult for some readers to identify with a hunter on safari in Africa, but it should not be difficult for them to relate the emotions of the man on safari with their own as they are in a similar hunting situation in their own territory. It's true that the quarry is relevant to the situation in many of the selections, but the feeling that's conveyed time and time again is that the important thing is the fact of the hunt—not the fact of the kill.

The editors' goal in assembling this collection was twofold. We hoped to get the very best hunting writers to bare their souls and tell their readers their most significant and memorable hunting experience. We also hoped, however, to provide a medium of understanding for nonhunters. It is our sincere wish that this book, through illustrative example, will help to explain what goes on in the mind of the hunter as he prepares to hunt and as he is hunting. The wish to express this thought was not explained to the contributors when their stories were solicited, however, because we believed that this feeling for the sport would be intrinsic in anything they wrote. Our belief is confirmed in the stories that follow.

Eric Peper
New City, New York
June 15, 1973

Hunting Moments of Truth

First Turkey

ED ZERN

If you should ever through some not likely but on the other hand not utterly inconceivable circumstance find yourself entered in a flatulence tournament, and if you accept that tenet of the competitive creed that anything worth doing is worth doing well, then by all means arrange to gorge yourself beforehand on prime zebra meat, preferably the backstrap; you will be a shoo-in to win in a breeze, so to speak. The meat of this equine is so rich that in the process of digestion it produces a vast cubic footage of sundry mists and vapors, all of startling pungency and so mephitic as to be hazardous in the vicinity of open fires.

I learned this because it is my practice to shoot nothing of which I do not intend to eat at least a portion, so that when I killed the three Burchell's zebra on my license while hunting near Lake Magadi with Denis Zaphiro, then Senior Warden of the Southern District of Kenya, and Wendell Swank, who once headed Arizona's fish-and-game department and is presently conducting pilot programs in game-cropping for the United Nations in East Africa, and having previously announced my no-eatum-no-shootum policy in a voice vibrant with equal parts of Glenlivet and righteousness, I was forthwith obliged to gnaw on broiled zebra until my jaws ached and the eyes of those downwind of me watered.

This is the principal reason, then, that most of my shooting is at creatures on the wing, as not only are they, in general, a more sporting proposition for the shooter but with the exception of such eminently edible ungulates as eland and gerenuk, and of course the delectable Tommy, they are likely to be a more satisfying proposition for the eater. And if the odd mallard or pintail proves to have been queer for clams or a veritable ancient among Anatidae, at least there is not half a ton of it on hand as in the case of an overly elderly elk or Methuselish moose.

(Two trips to East Africa have convinced me that big-game hunting is to bird-shooting as a Wagner overture is to a Mozart quartet—or, in the case of solitary woodcocking, perhaps, to a Bach suite for unaccompanied cello—and that by taste and inclination I am, in all such matters, a chamber-music type. True, I'd like some day to take a good Cape buffalo, and perhaps even a really fine greater kudu—but I doubt that any shot at such game, however well placed, could provide greater satisfaction than I've had from a clean-killed downhill grouse on a steep Pennsylvania mountainside or my one honest right-and-left on woodcock in a west-of-Ireland thicket. And although as I write this I'm planning a trip to the Ungava region of northern Quebec for caribou, I have as much pleasure in anticipating the ptarmigan shooting of that splendid region as in the prospect of reducing a reindeer to possession.)

And so, when invited last December to join a party of turkey hunters on a Texas ranch some hundred-odd miles west of San Antonio in Real County, I accepted, and went, although warned (by a very pretty lady, who had shot one) that wild gobblers are, chewability-wise, in a class with underdone innertubes.

My previous experience with Texas had consisted chiefly of a few days at the port of Galveston in the early thirties, while working as a merchant seaman, and of having lost an otherwise mint-condition tooth during a politico-philosophical discussion in an I.W.W. meeting hall, and so I was pleased to find, on arriving at the Rancho Real, that at least a portion of that sprawling state is rolling sand hills covered with pines and live oaks, well grassed and well watered, with deep ravines cut through the loose soil by clear-flowing creeks and rivers in whose bottomlands whitetail deer, wild turkey and a number of feral pigs find abundant cover.

In fact some of our party were more interested in deer than in turkeys, and I shall spare you and myself the embarrassment of describing my clean miss, one afternoon, of a standing ten-point whitetail at an easy 200 yards, although I have alibis as brilliantly inventive as any you've ever heard. But what most of us wanted was a turkey, especially those (including me) who had never shot one—even though I had been warned that not only are most gobblers in that area (as in most others) killed on the ground, but are even, sometimes, hunted with rifles.

And so I found myself, before dawn the next morning, crouched with another gunner, a local man, in a blind made of slabs of sandstone, open at one end and with crude log seats. By peering through the brush heaped high in front of the blind we could see, as dawn dispelled darkness, a baseball-diamond-sized clearing in the piny woods. It was, I'm sure, baited regularly (and quite legally), and before long my companion held finger to lips, and rolled his eyes toward the path behind us. Sure enough, I could hear a faint, almost mouselike scuffling in the pine needles, and when I turned my head very slowly I saw a flock of a dozen turkeys pussyfooting their way through the lingering mist, peering intently at every bush. Ten feet behind the blind the flock stopped, and one of the hens detached herself from the bunch, walked cautiously up to the open end of the blind, peered in at two motionless, breath-holding hunters (one of whom, at least, peered back) and slowly returned to the waiting flock.

When the old girl had whispered something to the others,

they turned and scampered back into the brush: end of turkey hunting that morning. We sat awhile, until the sun rose bright and hot, then fell back a long mile to the ranch house and regrouped.

Three days later there had been two deer killed and several missed, but nobody had got a turkey (although a famous wildlife artist in the group had had a shot at one feeding at fifty feet and, although I had seen him go 24/25 on his first attempt at skeet, had missed it cleanly: "Turkey fever?" he had said, in wonderment). But the weather, the whiskey and the company had been first-rate, and the countryside had been beautiful in a soft, un-Texan way, and when I turned in that night I was happy, although the hunt was ended.

In the morning we breakfasted at four-thirty, but at five our host said the cars to pick us up would be an hour late and urged us to relax and have more coffee. When I asked if he'd mind if I wandered back to that first-morning turkey blind, he whistled up a ranch hand with a pick-up truck, and off I went, wearing a business suit and clutching a Winchester Model 21 bored full and full and with half a dozen high-brass 4s in my pocket. It was still dark, but the driver dropped me at a path and said it led directly to the blind. I walked in and found it, then walked across the clearing, pulled some sticks into a heap in front of a live oak and sat behind the sticks with my back against the tree and my gun in my lap. It was lighter now, and I recalled our host declaiming on the remarkable eyesight of wild turkeys and especially the Rio Grande subspecies of that area. "A Rio Grande turkey," he had assured us (pronouncing it, proudly, *rye-oh*), "can see through a thin rock."

The lighter it got the more foolish I felt sitting virtually in the open, and when I had about decided to quit making a spectacle of myself and go get in the blind, I saw a movement across the clearing. It was a flock of about a dozen turkeys, tiptoeing cautiously up the same path I had come by and peering right and left. Ten feet behind the blind they stopped, and one of the hens walked cautiously to the open end of the blind and peered in. Then she walked happily back to the flock, which trotted out into the clearing and began scratching and feeding in the grass.

I expected at any moment to be spotted, especially after my nose started itching, but after a few minutes one of the darker-hued, short-bearded spring gobblers (which unlike the old gobblers run with the hens) detached itself from the bunch, and I shot it. This seemed to surprise the other turkeys, which got the hell out of there. Unlike the turkey killed by that pretty lady this young bird was delicate of flavor and texture, and my wife and I ate it for our Christmas dinner. It was far, far tastier and tenderer than zebra, and made me glad I had heeded my host's warning and not hid behind a thin rock.

The Hunt

NELSON BRYANT

There seems to be, when one looks back on nearly forty years of hunting, no particular incident that summons up its total meaning and magic. Images advance, recede and fade; still others, perhaps embellished by memory, assume an importance they may never have possessed. But if one persists, certain experiences emerge, each defining some aspect of the hunt with special clarity.

Consider the unspoken and close companionship that hunters together for the first time often feel. For me such a moment came on a searing morning in the Yucatán, when, my glasses adrift in a sea of sweat, I lurched over the rough terrain after a demented pointer that refused to hold the quail for more than five seconds before putting them to flight.

Ah, that was a dog: big, rangy and fleabitten, he hurtled through fields of sisal dragging several fathoms of rope behind him.

"Quick! Quick!" his handler shouted at me as soon as we set forth, indicating that I should stay on the animal's heels. I protested that there was no reason a hunter should cover all the ground a dog did, but in vain, for the handler had almost no English and I no Spanish.

A ragged entourage grew behind us as the morning progressed. Old men, young men and boys, all wearing white shirts, dark trousers, straw hats and sandals, they seemed to rise up from the earth, a magnificent and appreciative audience. They wanted to watch the Americans shoot—we were three guns—and they cheered each hit with wild delight and scurried out to pick up the birds.

Once after I took two quail from a covey rise and was breaking my gun to reload, a single bird burst from under my feet and flew away unscathed.

"Automatico! Automatico!" the gallery screamed, indicating that a double gun was too limiting.

We spent most of the morning hunting those wild, spooky birds, and by eleven o'clock were out of shells.

It was then that one of the group approached me, a small, smiling man of perhaps forty with a rusted single-barreled shotgun slung over his shoulder on a leather thong. Reaching into his pocket, he drew forth a single shell, the only one he had, and gave it to me. With the assistance of one of my companions who knew a little Spanish, I was given to understand that this was a gift with which I was to take one more quail.

The shell was so old I couldn't tell what load it contained, but I stuffed it in my gun and we headed back across the shimmering fields under a blazing sun.

A quarter of a mile later, the dog made point and I moved in. By ones, twos and threes, quail erupted on all sides of me until at least fifteen had taken wing, but none had offered a really certain shot and I did not want to miss.

Then no more birds rose, the dog moved away and my audience, fifty yards distant, was silent. I took one step and from behind me a single bird took flight. I slipped as I spun about on the uneven ground and the quail was forty yards away sliding down over the edge of a hill before I regained my balance and fired.

A few feathers drifted in the bright air after the bird fell and the gallery roared approval. The man with the gun retrieved the quail and brought it to me, doffing his hat and shaking my hand. I put my arm about his bony shoulders and there was no need for words.

And then there is the desire of every hunter to be a truly expert shot, a desire, if one is wise, that in later years becomes more closely attuned to reality, to one's actual ability, until a merely creditable performance, perhaps enlivened by occasional moments of luck or brilliance, will suffice.

I had been fishing for salmon on Robin Sinclair's holdings in Scotland's Caithness County, and the "Glorious Twelfth," the day in August when, for more than a century, the red grouse season opens, was fast approaching.

For more than a week I had listened to the restrained intonations of the English and Scottish anglers in the cozy dining room of Lochdhu Lodge, where a pungent peat fire always burned in the fireplace, but two days before the twelfth an ebullient party of shooting guests from the Continent arrived, French and Italian phrases flew about the room, and my excitement mounted.

Before the great day arrived, Sinclair, who is Lord Thurso, had shown me his grouse gun, a fine double Purdey that snapped shut with a solid assurance. And there was the gaunt, elderly and charming English gentleman who took me aside to observe with great displeasure that many of the Continental gunners had arrived with automatics, which he called abominations. He had learned that I was shooting a 20-gauge over-and-under Winchester—a fine gun, but certainly not in the Purdey's league. I also had the feeling that I would have been regarded more highly if the barrels of my Winchester had been side by side.

Leaving the gaunt Englishman, I met a British television

producer and we talked for half an hour outside the lodge in the strange late-evening twilight as mist collected on the moors. A magnificent stag and his hinds were stark against the sky on a low hill to the west, and the mountain called Moreven was a black hulk in the distance. We had both taken several brandies, so our talk was frank. "You damned American writers are every-where, aren't you?" he said. "But I'll give you credit, you don't sit on your duffs like our chaps and make believe you know the rest of the world. I suppose you're a crack shot?"

I replied, with what I thought was seemly reticence, that I was competent.

"There is one Italian dentist here, who, unlike most of them, shoots a double. He's so damned good he can often get his two birds, then reload and shoot a third on the same rise," my companion said in parting as we pushed open the massive oak doors of the lodge and went inside.

That night Lord Thurso informed me that he had arranged a beat for me to shoot and that I would have a gamekeeper to handle the dogs and a ghillie with me, the latter, I learned, to carry extra shells and the downed birds.

In some areas of Scotland, one shoots driven grouse, birds that are set flying toward hunters at specific shooting locations, or butts. At Lochdhu it was walk-up shooting. One used setters or pointers as one does for quail. This would be, I thought hope-fully, to my advantage, for I had done a good deal of upland bird shooting in my own country.

The following morning an intermittent fine rain swept across the heather and Lord Thurso called and said, "My game-keeper is ill. I'll handle the dogs for you."

An hour later I was slogging across the lumpy moor terrain behind Lord Thurso and his dogs, and, because he is a vigorous, stalwart man, the pace was merry.

"What in hell," I mused at one point, "am I, a New Eng-land country boy, doing in this wild and lovely place with a gun in my hand and a viscount as my guide? What if I shoot poorly? But how can I shoot poorly? The birds are large and no faster than the ruffed grouse back home, and there are no trees, no bushes, nothing they can fly behind."

The first brace of grouse rose cackling on my right about thirty yards away and seemed to be slow fliers until their wings caught the wind. I fired once and didn't touch a feather. Lord Thurso, a perfect gentleman, said nothing, but a vision of the deadly Italian dentist, somewhere on the same moor, dropping birds right and left, rose before me. I missed once again, and despite the chilling rain, began to sweat. On my next opportunity I downed a single bird with one shot, but he was not killed cleanly.

The wizened little ghillie murmured compassionately as he showed me the bird before dropping it into his cavernous game bag, "You're taking too long, sir. That one was fifty yards away when you shot."

Then it happened. The dogs located a covey. A dozen or more grouse rose against the gray sky and I scored a clean double before they were six feet off the ground. "Good work!" the laird cried, and one of his sons, who was also shooting, brought me a sprig of rare white heather he had found—for good luck, he said. The wind died, the sun emerged, I was relaxed and content, and from that point on my shooting was competent.

No hunting experience has been more memorable than the wild November day my brother Dan, my brother-in-law Bob Morgan, and I went forth for black ducks on a remote Martha's Vineyard beach.

Snow had been falling half the night when Bob called early in the morning to say that it was a proper day for black ducks. The specific location shall remain nameless, for it cannot stand much hunting pressure.

When we reached the outer beach along the Vineyard's south shore, the snow, driven by a northwest gale, was a swirling, writhing shroud that often limited our vision to a few feet.

Our trip along the narrow strip of beach, with salt ponds on one side of us and the gray, heaving ocean on the other, was difficult, and even though we were using four-wheel drive we bogged down twice and had to dig and push our way free. The second time we were stuck we realized that the storm had increased in intensity and that there was a good chance we would not get back if we continued on.

Turning back, we found after traveling a quarter of a mile

that our outgoing tracks were obliterated by the drifting snow, but just as we reached our starting point the sky lightened, a tiny slice of blue appeared, the snow stopped and in half an hour the howling, moaning wind, gusting sixty miles an hour or more, tore the clouds from the sky.

"It couldn't be better," said Bob. "The tide is right. The snow is over. Let's go back."

Although we had already spent two hours on the beach, we once again turned around and eventually reached the spot where we planned to shoot, a narrow peninsula with a shallow tidal pool about sixty yards long and twenty yards wide in its center.

We put six black duck decoys in the pool and huddled in some wild rose bushes at its edge with the biting gale at our backs. Four decoys would have been enough, but we added the other two for good measure.

In the next half hour the temperature fell ten or fifteen degrees and the wind continued unabated, then five black ducks came low over the white-capped waters of the salt pond that lay on the south side of our peninsula, headed for the decoys and the bushes that partially obscured Dan and me. Bucking the gale, they were scarcely able to make headway, their ground speed probably not much more than ten miles an hour.

Under normal circumstances, the natural blinds we were using would have been inadequate, for the black is one of the wariest of ducks, but in a high wind they often seem to lose their caution, becoming, as Bob puts it, "Gallied."

"When they get over the decoys, you take the lead birds and I'll take the two in the rear," I said to Dan.

At the instant they were above the decoys, the three rearward ducks spied us and flared away. I swung on the second of the two lead birds and fired, but a split second before that I heard Dan's gun cough once and both birds were falling at the precise moment I shot.

"They crossed as I was getting on them and I couldn't resist," Danny said, grinning. That bit of one-upmanship ended his shooting, for two is the limit, and less than fifteen minutes later Bob and I had taken our two birds each also.

Although our shooting was done, we remained for an hour watching flight after flight of blacks, sometimes only two birds, sometimes more than a dozen, come to our decoys, necks out-stretched and powerful wings stroking the turbulent air. At times, if we remained seated, they came so close we could see every detail of their feathers.

Then the outgoing tide sucked the pool dry, and, numbed almost beyond feeling, we retrieved our ice-covered decoys and sat in our wind-rocked Jeep sharing a thermos of coffee as the brilliant late-afternoon sunlight gleamed on a wild winter scene.

"The black duck is the very best waterfowl of them all," I said, and my companions did not dissent.

The Wait and the Shot

JIM CARMICHEL

The circumstances which led to my personal moment of truth began with the black root. Black root is a disease which attacks and destroys young tobacco plants while they are still in their incubation period. The disease apparently is held in the soil of previous tobacco beds, or perhaps it is airborne. I don't know. At any rate it seems that when one farmer's beds are stricken so are lots of other farmers'. Naturally this wreaks great economic hardship throughout the burley belt where I lived as a youngster. Without healthy plants there would be no tobacco crop, and tobacco was the area's leading source of cash money in those days.

Like most farm lads of that time and place I raised a small bed of plants each spring in the hopes that some burley grower would come up short on his own beds and have to buy mine. This would usually net me somewhere in the neighborhood of ten to fifteen dollars. No small sum in those days, for only two months' work. I was not allowed to use any of my family's cleared land, but I was allowed to clear a small area in the woods and use that.

As it came to pass, this protected bit of virgin soil was one of the few surviving beds one year when the black root struck particularly hard. Of course I didn't have enough plants for all the panic-stricken farmers, but I did have enough to save one or two from complete disaster. Needless to say the bidding for my bed of plants was somewhat spectacular. When the bids soared over one hundred dollars I was overcome with the giddiness and sense of power that comes only with extreme wealth.

When the final bid was in, and accepted, I found myself with enough cold, hard cash to buy myself a Winchester Model 70 rifle in .270 caliber, a 2.5 × scope, a genuine leather gun case, and about two hundred rounds of ammunition. Everything, I supposed, I'd ever want for the rest of my life. . . .

One factor I'd overlooked, however, was exactly how I'd make use of the rifle and all that ammo. Deer had been scarce in that area for half a century, the nearest moose was a thousand miles away and the nearest elk at least twice that far. They may as well have been on the moon.

But I didn't despair. A year before the likelihood of my owning such a fine rig had been about as conceivable as my ascension to the chairmanship of Standard Oil. I had at least learned that nothing is impossible. In the meantime I consoled myself by cleaning the rifle about two times a day and occasionally sending a 150-grain slug through an eight-inch stump—to the considerable awe of my pals. Then tragedy struck.

I had improvised a gun rack of sorts by driving a couple of pegs in my bedroom wall. One day one of the pegs gave way and the rifle fell. The stock was split clear through at the grip. Tears.

A new stock, I learned, would cost about thirty dollars, and I was broke again. More tears.

Who, I wondered, in all history, had endured such misery? Job? Probably not. Bonaparte at Waterloo? Not even close. My agony was unique. This, I believed, was fate's way of telling me that a hunter I was not to be. I would never set the crosshairs on a royal elk, clatter along a shale slide after a bighorn, or even have my picture taken with a record-book antelope.

Just about the time my despair was complete a second miracle occurred. My shop teacher, Russell Shadoan, a gun nut of the first water and something of a gunsmith, took pity on me and suggested that I undertake to build a rifle stock as my term shop project. It would be a tough project for a dumb kid like me, but if I would give it a try he would help all he could.

Would I try!

That term I sawed, knifed, chiseled, scraped, sanded, rubbed and polished like a person possessed by demons. I shed enough blood to stock a bloodbank, dripped enough sweat to float a canoe and smeared enough Prussian blue on my good school clothes to paint six masterpieces. But I made a stock! It wasn't much of a stock, I guess, but I thought it was beautiful. The finish was hand-rubbed oil, there was a cheekpiece, and I even *painted* the tip of the fore-end black so it would look like the custom rifles I'd seen in pictures.

Too, while working on the stock, I'd done some realistic thinking about my hunting future. There weren't any bears, elk or moose nearby, and there were so few deer that I wasn't likely to see one if I hunted a lifetime. In time perhaps I would be able to journey to the fabled lands where game was said to abound, but that was years away. There *were*, however, worthy targets close at hand. Crows were everywhere, and I heard that woodchucks could be found in some nearby areas.

Local farming practices had all but eliminated woodchucks (we called 'em groundhogs) in our immediate area. In fact, their decimation had been so total that I had seen only two or three in my life. There were quite a few to be found on the mountain slopes, however, and Mr. Shadoan promised me a trip to a place he knew about as soon as the school term ended.

A trip to deepest Africa could not have been prepared for

more carefully nor with greater anticipation. With no money, but some great luck, I managed to trade the 2.5× scope for a real varmint scope of a mighty 10 power, and the remaining ammunition I had on hand was swapped for fast, flat-shooting .270 loads with 110-grain bullets.

With these improvements to work with I set out in earnest to really learn how to shoot that rifle. Firing at targets placed at different ranges, I learned how much a bullet drops at long range, how wind affects the flight of a bullet, how accurate the rifle and ammo really were and what size target I could expect to hit at any given range. Still, what with the heartbreaking luck I'd had with the busted stock and all, I couldn't help being a bit discouraged about my future hunting prospects. One thing for sure, though: when the time came to find out I intended to be ready. . . .

The big day was a bright and warm Saturday in late May. During the drive into the mountains I persuaded Mr. Shadoan to stop and let me try a couple of "sighters" just to make sure the sights were set exactly. Frankly, considering my past luck, I doubted getting even one shot, but in case I did, I did not want to blow it for Mr. Shadoan and the whole world to see.

The area where we went was high sheep pasture. There were few trees and almost no brush, only lush grass, spotted here and there with granite outcroppings. Here and there were chuck dens a foot or more across, but no chucks. Not even one. According to what I had read and heard about chuck hunting, one could shoot until his gun barrel got too hot to touch. But here I was in supposedly good chuck country and, just as I had secretly suspected, there wasn't a groundhog anywhere. But I was determined to make the best of an otherwise pleasant trip and not let Mr. Shadoan know how disappointed I was. "Some people are born hunters and some aren't," I reasoned, "but when I try even the woodchucks leave."

Mr. Shadoan, who didn't seem concerned in the least about the absence of chucks, directed me to climb to the top of the steep ridge so I could get a good view of several dens at once. In the meantime he would cross another ridge and check what lay beyond.

At the crest of the ridge I rolled my jacket into a ball to serve as a shooting rest, took up a fairly comfortable prone position, located all the dens within possible range and began what I was sure would be a futile vigil.

For the first hour or so there was nothing. I moved the scope from den to den until I knew the exact shape of each, plus every pebble and every twig around them. But no matter how many times I looked, or how hard I looked, they were always the same—empty. All, that is, except one. It was one of the farthest out, about 300 yards I reckoned, and thus the hardest to make out any detail. But something looked different—like a pointed rock at the entrance.

I looked at that odd shape for a full ten minutes or more and it remained absolutely motionless. I had about decided that it was nothing more than a rock I'd failed to note before, when suddenly it moved! Not a big movement, mind you. Just a slight forward motion.

It's alive!

A groundhog!

But where's the rest of it?

I could still see only the tip of the nose, not even the eyes. Certainly not enough to shoot at. Nonetheless I flipped the safety off, opened the bolt and took the cartridge out of the chamber. With the chamber empty I could "dry-fire" at the chuck's nose and check my hold and trigger squeeze.

At first my heart pounded so that the crosshairs did a crazy dance at least as wide as the whole den. After a while, though, I calmed down enough to pretty well hold on what little bit of woodchuck I could see. All I needed to do now was play it cool and wait until the chuck came completely out and I'd have a pretty good chance of making a hit. So with surprising calm I went about reviewing what I'd have to do.

The 110-grain bullet loads I was using had been sighted in so that they printed an inch and a half above point of aim at a hundred yards. I knew from my practice sessions that this would put the point of impact about four inches low at the range I estimated the chuck to be. But I also knew that the bullet's trajectory began falling off so rapidly beyond 300 yards that the bullet would fall about five more inches below the line of sight in the next fifty yards.

So an error in range estimation could mean hitting too low. Just how much room for error I'd have depended on whether or not the chuck would stand up when he came completely out, or if he would remain on all fours.

By this time I could see all of his head but nothing more. He seemed to be snoozing and not intending to come out any farther at all. What's more, the thought occurred to me that when Mr. Shadoan came back the chuck would spot him and disappear completely.

So the choice became agonizingly simple. I could wait for the chuck to come on out, which he didn't appear likely to do. This would give me a better target and I'd run the risk of him being frightened into the den. Or I could try for the head shot and hope that my range estimation and aim were close enough.

At least it would be a clean hit or a clean miss. So I snapped off a couple more dry "shots" at a spot just over his head and slipped a round into the chamber.

I can only vaguely remember sighting or pulling the trigger, but I remember in stark clarity looking at the den after shooting and seeing nothing but the empty hole. No sign of the chuck.

Assuming I had missed but determined at least to know how close I'd come, I climbed down the steep side of the ridge and up the facing hillside where the den was.

When I got to the den I found that rather than tunneling straight back into the hillside it angled downward for a couple of feet, and that's where that grizzled old groundhog—a .270 bullet hole just under his right eye—had dropped.

Bonasa umbellus monticola NÖEL

GEORGE BIRD EVANS

Certain gun dogs are star-marked for disaster by something that pursues them through whatever years they know of life. Some of them make it to old age; others aren't so lucky. Briar, a slashing orange belton fifth-generation of our Old Hemlock line (for the first time in twenty-five years the only setter we had), was one of two survivors in a litter of seven where this thing began. Through the generosity of a friend, we got him at a time when our strain appeared destined for extinction.

As a young dog, he was attacked by a ninety-five-pound

crossbred Great Dane–boxer, retired from canine police duty to a back-country mountain farm. The heavyweight was clubbed off before too much blood was shed and before Briar's spirit was dampened, but Kay and I were shaken.

Collisions with barbed wire left marks until Briar learned to take fences like a hunter. On his first woodcock hunt, we lost him in the hugeness of West Virginia's Canaan Valley. I found him hours later, trailing deer. Until his predilection for deer scent was corrected, overnight absences had us living with fear of road hazards and trigger-happy sheep farmers, but Briar came through.

One ugly experience took place in a wild valley in our Alleghenies where Kay and I were gunning this past November. The irony of these situations was that Briar seemed unaware of danger. Working from the headwaters, we were intent upon his quartering through hemlock and rhododendron, and came unexpectedly to a board shanty in a cluster of derelict cars—a scene to delight any sociologist. A scurry of chickens from behind the wrecks alerted me and I blew my whistle for Briar, who came promptly. A gray, wiry little man came into view from the dooryard, headed for what I took to be a late-afternoon hunt, carrying a double-barreled hammer gun. He ignored my greeting and walked toward a hog lot where he bent over and picked up a large white chicken, dangling it by one leg as I approached.

"Did my dog do that?" I asked, watching the hen blinking up at him.

"If I'd got here sooner there wouldn't be no dog." He sounded disappointed.

"You wouldn't shoot a dog for a chicken," I said, not too convinced. "It doesn't appear hurt, but I'll pay you for it." I handed him a bill. "Why don't you put it in that shed and see if it recovers?"

The chicken was watching him with its upside-down blinking stare, as though awaiting the verdict, but the man didn't indicate he heard me. Laying it on a chopping block, he took a blunt ax and sent the head rolling to the ground, still blinking in disbelief. I honestly think the little bastard enjoyed doing it, and it was not until we were a quarter of a mile away that I realized how close we had come to losing Briar on what had been up to then a wonderful autumn afternoon.

For Kay and me, white Christmases hold no charm. We open our gifts like other people in Abercrombie & Fitch's Christmas catalog, dressed in shooting clothes. If weather is fit, by afternoon we are in a favorite grouse covert.

We live in a singularly unspoiled portion of the Appalachians. Unlike the more spectacularly high mountains to the south of us, our area has escaped the attention of "recreation" planners and drowses on in a nineteenth-century tempo, with a few of the older houses, like our own, preserving the mood of a hundred years before that. Almost the only industrial imprint is left by the probing snout of the stripe-mine shovel that unwittingly creates game cover with the high-wall and spoil-bank edges—not too obstrusive with present-day reclamation laws. That same shovel rooted out families who "sold the coal rights" and whose new houses and mobile homes punctuate the highways at night with their dusk-to-dawn lights. This gives a false impression of population, for many of these squatting habitats represent countless abandoned farms in the backlands where woodland crowds into fields going wild.

In our once-great grouse coverts the birds have become disturbingly scarce. Cover has changed—often favorably and, overall, it is nearly as choice as ever. But where it was once normal to find twelve to fifteen grouse in a half day, it now takes hard hunting and good luck to move four or five, and only if you have a moderately wide, industrious grouse dog who knows his business.

Christmas Day 1972 was without snow—a lovely cool, damp, cloudy forty-three degrees, perfect scenting temperature. The place we had saved for this hunt is a rounded knob, rising like an enormous mound from a flatland of hawthorns, and today we shared the covert with a solitary hound questing mournfully in the far reaches. The hill is old pasture grown to hawthorns on the west and on top, with hardwoods on the east and tangles of wild grapevines bordering a mud road. There is an alder glade in the bottom—a honey of a 'cock covert during the flights—and along the west slope a strip-mine scar has filled with spring water to form a lake about 150 feet wide, nearly a half-mile long and God knows how deep. It is the only man-made mark since the last farm buildings rotted away thirty years ago.

Into this gem of a place I cast Briar in a maze of gun-barrel gray thorns under a grayer sky and Kay and I followed. The first grouse, wind-nervous, lifted well in front of Briar and headed for the hardwoods on top. Swinging to the western slope, we soon had two good points but the birds were equally uneasy there. Following the second bird, we heard Briar's bell go quiet in a low thicket where we found him solid. Kay stopped to take movies of the point while I circled, keeping in the opening between the cover and the strip mine in case the grouse should come out that way. The slope was so steep, Briar's head in the thorns above me was lower than his rump and nearly straight-up tail. Kay, her camera to her eye, had gone on her knees to give me the shot if the grouse should climb. The only flaw in a grand situation was that no bird materialized.

I pushed my way into the thorny branches directly toward Briar, who held like a saint, his eyes bulging, one orange-flecked ear stirred by the breeze. I shuffled, left foot forward, in front of him, my pulse almost double, and when nothing happened, gave him the low two-note whistle to move on. At his step, a spot within feet of where I'd passed on the outside erupted and a grouse went straight off the slope without rising. My pattern caught it halfway across the clearing but momentum carried the bird, streaming feathers, over the edge of the strip mine and out of sight. I swelled with the savage elation of a hit over a point, heightened by the string of misses that had agonized me of late, and Kay's joyful exclamation behind me seemed to come from my throat.

Briar and I reached the brink of the high wall together, and I started down with eyes reacting to the change of plane. On green water more than thirty feet below, I saw a scattering of feathers, then the floating grouse. Thrashing wings pulled it under headfirst like a diving duck, before it became immobile and floated belly-up. As I watched, faced with the loss of my grouse, the water bloomed with showering shale and Briar hit the surface with a plunge so deep it took moments for him to come up and begin swimming. He seemed confused until he saw the bird, then paddled to it and grasped it in grand retriever fashion and started back. In its last paroxysm, the grouse fluttered free of his mouth just as he reached the vertical wall and in that instant I could see his realization that he was in trouble.

Most dogs swim instinctively, the way Briar had always

done in moderately shallow trout streams, retrieving or simply crossing, and after the shock of seeing him go over the high wall I felt no real concern, for he had scaled some of these like a mountain goat. But this time he seemed worried, abandoning the grouse and scrambling for a foothold at the base of the sheer rock, where he lost his balance and went out of sight under the water. Kay and I crept closer to the edge and saw two areas of muddy turbulence deep down and spreading into clear water. I heard Kay's shrill, "My God, I don't see him!" and in the awful quiet, my brain churned the image of words on a Christmas card, telling of a pointer bitch lost "in a freak hunting accident" in strip-mine country, and the memory of a local Brittany killed in a fall over a high wall.

In the world of the hunter, death is not supposed to reach the other way. Babbling commonplaces, I stupidly removed my belt as if I could possibly reach Briar down in that ice-cold water, having the sense to not plunge in after him, and lacking the guts. I don't know how long this lasted. It came to an end with the most glorious sound I have heard—Briar's bell somewhere out of sight and shale rattling into the water from the vertical high wall. He almost made it, then crashed back down. We could hear him swimming and the rhythm sounded tired. When he came into view the cold water was slowing him but he struck for the far shore, a diminishing shape as he got farther away. At last he reached the gentle slope and dragged himself wearily out of the water and shook—that wonderful bell sound carrying across to us.

It would have made a great story if I could relate that Briar had carried the grouse to land and, as he did now at my hand signal, raced around the end of the lake to us, but neither Briar nor I are heroes. Kay and I were silent in our relief at having our arms around his wet neck, as he struggled, impatient to hunt.

A grouse gunner's mind quickly reverts to grouse after almost anything that can happen. Following the brink of the high wall to the southern end, we moved downhill and along the far shore where we pondered my bird, long since dead, bobbing in the wind-ruffled water near the base of the high wall. It had drifted several yards in the lengthwise direction of the lake but there was no hope that the breeze would carry it to our side. A wasted grouse is a disappointing experience, no matter how little you can blame yourself.

At three p.m. we gave up trying to think of a way to reach it, and moved into the big flats in the bottom. We had an interesting hunt, bathed in a sensation of relief. Briar pointed a covey of five bobwhites with several productives on singles (I didn't care to shoot any from so small a covey); we saw fresh woodcock splashings in the glade, surprising at this late date; jumped two whitetails; and Briar pointed a brace of grouse, one of which I missed with some bitterness, for I wanted a grouse badly.

About five o'clock, we were once again near the strip-mine lake, and with an unreasoning hope of finding my dead grouse, we began a careful examination along the only side we could reach. There was no trace of it on the edge or afloat, and as we climbed around the north end where the contour of the hill merged with the high wall, I wondered how soon a bird would sink. In the failing light, I could see something floating just beneath the surface but it proved to be a water-logged rabbit with fur turned an unfamiliar blue. From this end I noticed, for the first time, a tiny ravine that was the only break in the long high wall where it was possible to reach the water. Approaching it, I could make out a silhouette like driftwood or coal shale at the water's edge. Kay cried out as I stumbled toward it and I scarcely believe it yet. Our dead grouse lay floating with its tail feathers folded, its head toward the shore. Carried by wind-drift, it had lodged in the one accessible place in the more than quarter-mile of shore along which it had floated during the past two hours. With meticulous caution, I reached for the form, feeling it might still elude me.

We stood there in the dusk, Kay and I, laughing hys·terically and hooting like two inebriates. When we heard Briar's bell coming toward us, I laid the soaking bird on the bank and whistled. He found it, looking bewildered, then picked it up and insisted upon carrying it around before relinquishing it, his grin as wide as ours.

As we climbed the hillside above the water, a grouse flushed and sailed down past me. Instinctively I started the mount, then lowered the little Purdey still on *safe*. I am shooting at no more birds where they might fall into strip-mine lakes. When at last we reached the station wagon, all that was left of another Christmas day was a streak of opalescent green under clouds in the southwest, and a wet grouse—not its handsomest, but beautiful to Kay and Briar and me. During recent years, I

Bonasa umbellus
monticola
NÖEL

27

have longed for the days when I knew grouse in plenty, when in these coverts a dog could have over a hundred productive points in a month and a half of gunning. There are parts of northern grouse range where such numbers can be found today. But I'm not sure the scarcity I deplore hasn't enriched my shooting, as long as I can gun these lovely coverts that are so much my own. To me, each ruffed grouse I shoot has become an experience almost mystical, enhanced by the point, the retrieve, the setting, cherished as a single happening that would be dulled by numbers.

It is not altogether true to tell that this afternoon's hunt ended on that back road with the wet feathers of that grouse cold under my fingers. Moments such as this—and those of us who gun know them well—do not end with the moment but are with us from that moment on. On nights when sleep is slow to come, I see again two murky spots deep in green water, and listen for a bell that does not ring.

The Painful Moose

CLARE CONLEY

Hunts are memorable for many reasons—your first and, worse luck, your last; the most exciting; the most dangerous; the biggest trophy; the happiest; the one with special friends; and more. They can occur anywhere from a small-game thicket in the back pasture to a mountain in Tibet, and, of course, they can happen anytime. You most often only really know how great one was long after it is over.

But of all the memorable hunts I have had in near places

and far and for whatever reasons, one that stands out in my memory occurred in Alaska in the fall of 1971. And the reason I remember it so well is the strange collection of things which happened to all of us, but mostly to me. I guess I'd have to say the reason I remember it is that there seemed to be no reason at all to the unusual collection of occurrences. And surprisingly I know I would have to rate it as the most painful hunt I was ever on.

On September 4, Fred Bear, the father of modern-day bow-hunting, Colonel Joe Engle, the astronaut who will pilot our first space shuttle in years to come, and I arrived at Bob Buzby's hunting camp on the Dry Creek, eighty miles by air south of Fairbanks, Alaska.

Since this was my first time in Alaska for hunting, and because I had read about it so much, I hurried to get started at the soonest opportunity on the first afternoon. But whereas I had expected to see big game, moose and caribou, everywhere, I soon learned that Alaska on foot is even larger than it looks on the map and game animals are not found in each and every little clump of willows and side draws. For the most part my afternoon became a kind of get-acquainted-with-the-area affair in which I learned that a mountain which looks close and easy to walk over is usually miles away and a tough climb.

The next day, now knowing better what to expect, I got away from camp early and alone, and with my bow clutched in my hand I left behind in the first hour the area I had poked around in the first afternoon out. In the meanwhile Joe Engle had elected to go for a Dall sheep with a rifle as his first choice and packed on out to a camp higher up in the mountains. Although we later kept daily contact with that camp by radio it would be a week before Joe returned with his trophy. Fred on that first day chose to scout some natural salt licks for fresh activity and to build blinds. He of all of us knew what he was doing.

I can't really do justice to describing what it is like to walk across a rolling sidehill in that part of Alaska. The slopes are covered with low brush, shin-high mostly, with occasional lines of taller brush along the route of every trickle of water. The valley bottoms are lined with evergreens, softwoods and willows, but the mountainsides are mostly short brush. And on these slopes I set off for some little rolling hills in the distance which looked promising. An hour later I didn't seem to be gaining on them much. A second hour's walking did make a noticeable difference, and while glassing the area where I was going during a rest stop I saw, wonder of wonders, what I considered to be a nice caribou. He was wandering without apparent motive in and around three little knobs which were strung out in a line. The same knobs had caught my eye when I first saw them at the start of the day.

I'd like to say that I performed a miraculous stalk on that bull caribou across the mile or so of open ground that separated us right to an eyeball-to-eyeball confrontation. And actually I didn't do too badly—except that the caribou didn't know or care where he was going and consequently never went in the same direction more than a minute or two, and he never stopped either. Finally I knew I had him figured out. I had cut the distance to the knobs down to a couple hundred yards, and when he went out of sight behind Knob No. 1 heading for Knob No. 3, I raced across the last open flat intent on Ambush at Knob No. 3. I got there, got in position to draw and waited—and waited. Finally I decided I would chance a little peek around the knob just to find out what was taking the bull so long. All I saw was the tail end of a caribou vanishing in the wrong direction around the first knob. I charged around Knobs 3 and 2 and cut in between Knobs 2 and 1 for another interception. And there I was fooled again. The wandering caribou was now out in the flat a hundred yards watching me run crazily around. Finding that dull stuff, he started feeding and walking on up the mountain, not particularly concerned. At that moment I realized I had just as much chance of running into that bull caribou by going in the opposite direction as I did by following him. And I may have run into him again sometime for all I know, but how can you tell. Most of them look alike.

Anyway I started back down the little line of knobs, which actually were on the crest of a draw that led down to one of the main creeks in the drainage. Only they were back from the creek a half-mile or so and were maybe 400 feet higher. Heavy tall brush grew up the slope from the creek, and by sneaking along at the crest I could scout the whole thing pretty well. This I was carrying off in style when I nearly ran into a moose lying in my path. Instantly I dropped to my knees so I could be out of sight and look things over better. Then I realized it was just a calf moose and he was asleep.

But, I told myself—someone had to—if a baby moose is there, nearby a papa moose with big antlers might be hiding too. So I tippytoed back the way I came, went out of sight over the crest, and sneaked back in beyond where the calf was dozing. Then all hell broke loose. The calf got up about twenty yards away and stood and looked at me, but below a big moose got up from a bed in a standing broad jump that took it almost out of sight instantly. All I saw was the back end of an adult moose which looked like it was trying to cut around me to get over the crest.

Running for all I was worth on the muskeg and brush, I circled back around a low rise to the next logical pass where the moose might come out. My feet were as light as feathers as I raced over the muskeg—about like running on a mattress. I had it made, too, until one of those light feet hooked something. I remember a rather spectacular arching trajectory through the air, and then I hit, left arm holding my bow away, right arm extended over my head. Instantly my right shoulder plowed down in the soft muskeg, wrenching my right arm back in a way it is not meant to go.

I remember crawling back into a standing position and doing a mental checklist of all my working parts. Nothing seemed too bad. I had a funny feeling in my right shoulder, though, rather like all the muscles in it had been stretched to the ripping point and then let snap back. Then I tried to lift it. The grating, crunching, and popping was unbelievable. I put it down, rubbed it for a moment, and raised it once more. Again it sounded like a rock crusher at work. It didn't hurt much just then, but I didn't need a fortuneteller to inform me trouble was coming. And to make matters even more impossible, the moose never did come out the way I expected. He ran straight downhill, and as I was fitting my parts back together, I saw him run out in the open at the bottom—and he turned out to be a she anyway, a big cow. My first non-reason event!

I had a long walk back, and by now most of the day was used up so I went downhill to the creek which flowed into another creek that Buzby's camp was on. Along the way I took several shots at ptarmigan without hitting one, and to this day I am still amazed that I could pull the 55-pound-draw bow.

I got back to camp just in time for dinner, and by then my shoulder was aching steadily and getting worse. Fred had investigated several salt licks and although it seemed as if he wasn't hunting much, it was now obvious to me that setting up blinds near places the caribou and moose would frequent was the only practical way to hunt. He also learned that the main migration from summer range to winter range of the caribou had not come through, and that the moose were not rutting and doing all the silly things that go with it as yet.

The next morning after a pained erratic sleep, I found it was impossible to move my arm more than an inch away from my side. The pain was so intense that all the strength in my right shoulder was gone and the arm just hung uselessly at my side. That was a fine fix for a bowhunter to be in at the beginning of a hunt. All day long I spent heating sand on the wood stove in the tent Fred and I shared and then putting it in a plastic bag and packing it on my shoulder. That helped the pain and by the end of the day I could move my arm slightly. But I was still a long way from being able to hunt. I had two choices. I could fly out to Fairbanks to a doctor or try to luck it out on the chance it would get better.

I elected to stay on at Dry Creek. Even without hunting it was still one of the most beautiful places I have ever been. Even now I would rather be there with a shoulder that hurts like hell than in a hospital bed in Fairbanks with nurses jabbing me with painkillers.

Fred had much the same attitude. It was just being there that counted. For several days I just poked around camp and the nearby woods, something that most hunters never take time to do. And it was great. I saw ptarmigan and snowshoe rabbits, I found wolf skulls, and generally got a lot more out of the trip than I might have otherwise. Fred hunted a little and messed around with me a lot.

Each day I was working on getting my shoulder so I could use it again. I had some cortisone and that helped. I got my arm to the point where I could raise it about shoulder high, but it still cracked and crunched a lot and had no strength. I had to get it back to something like full mobility quickly, and so I started taking a small rope and throwing it over a cross piece in the center of our cabin, and then by wrapping it around my right hand I would slowly draw the arm up by pulling down on the rope with my left hand. It was torture the first time or two, but after a while it did seem to help my injured shoulder.

After about a week of our two-week hunt I decided to try a short rabbit hunt with Fred. I could draw the bow back but not all the way, which is necessary for aiming and power. Needless to say I didn't hit a single rabbit, but at least I was hunting. Fred on the other hand was a real Indian at rabbit hunting and bagged several. I remember once he stopped as we were chasing rabbits through the willows and remarked that we were hunting rabbits at $150 a day per person, but it sure was fun. And it was.

Fred also liked to ride and took long tours of the surrounding mountains. On one of these afternoons he returned to camp with the casual information that he had just shot a bull moose. But that was a story unto itself no matter how he tended to make it seem a trifle. He had been riding his favorite horse and had come out on a promontory of one hill where he stopped to look things over. Across a small valley where a plateau crested before the terrain dropped down to the creek he saw two cow moose and one nice bull. It was midday and they were feeding in the willows just at the break of the plateau. Actually it was not far from where I had hurt my shoulder.

The bull obviously was interested in other things as well as willows, for he was raking every tall willow he came to with his antlers and in moose language this is as much as saying, "I'm pretty tough and anytime you two girls feel like getting on with propagating the species, I'm ready." They weren't ready, but he was bent on hanging around until they were. All this Fred understood.

After eating a while, the moose bedded down for a noonday nap, which gave Fred a chance to ride to the creek, tie up his horse, and sneak up the hillside below the moose as close as he dared. Below the willows at the crest of the hill was open low brush for about a hundred yards down to the last bit of cover, a clump of dead willows about the diameter of a bushel basket. Fred managed to sneak to this cluster of willows, but he could go no farther, so he waited.

After an hour or so the cows began to stir, and soon they

came out of the lower edge of the willows, heading for a natural salt lick along the creek more or less in Fred's direction. They passed within a few yards as they meandered down. But the bull didn't come, so Fred stayed.

Fred told me later he figured the bull would eventually discover the cows were gone and go after them. And sure enough after a while he rose from his bed, looked around, thrashed a few more willows, and started downhill, on the same trail the cows had used. Fred got ready.

Then just as the bull was about to pass he spied the clump of willows behind which Fred was hiding. Turning off the trail, he headed straight for them, obviously intent on working them over with his antlers. At thirteen steps, Fred decided that was close enough and stood up. The bull stopped in surprise and that was enough time for Fred to shoot. The moose turned, went fifty yards in a few seconds and fell dead.

That night Joe returned with a good Dall sheep which he had earned by days of arduous stalking high up in the mountains, and the next afternoon in contrast to his difficult sheep hunting, he spotted a moose on a hillside above camp, stalked it and shot it with a rifle all within an hour or so.

Days now passed uneventfully with each of us hunting in his own way. I could now draw my bow completely, but painfully, and so I spent my time in blinds at natural salt licks. Caribou and moose came within scant yards of my hiding place, but not ones that I wanted. So I took pictures and waited. Nothing. We extended our hunt a week, knowing that as soon as the first cold weather came many animals would move through the valley.

Finally the next to the last day arrived. We decided that on that day we would cross a high ridge and hunt in the next valley over from camp, perhaps five miles away but a difficult climb and walk in muskeg. That's where the caribou were. Hundreds of them were in the open flats of the valley. We scattered, each trying to find a way to get near the animals. Nothing I tried seemed to work. I was always in the wrong place and out in the open. Joe had gone down along the creek where a line of trees provided concealment behind which he could walk, and sure enough late in the day I heard him shoot. He was then a mile or two farther from camp than I was, and I remember wondering how he could take care of the meat and get the trophy back to camp. I wasn't even certain of his exact location, he was that far away.

Evening was coming and I had a long walk back across muskeg, which is difficult crossing even in the light. Mixed in with the low brush which drags at your legs are endless numbers of small potholes the size of a bathtub and smaller. These must be avoided because although some are shallow, some are deep and filled with mud. It's frustrating in the daytime and a nightmare in the dark. Also there was always the climb back over the mountain to consider.

After waiting as long as I could and watching for anyone else, I finally gave up and started back. It was dark before I reached camp. Everyone was there but Joe.

We had a drink while we waited. Occasionally one of us would step outside the cabin to shine a light and yell. No answer. Would he stay out all night? We doubted it. Could he find his way in the dark through the mountains and in the muskeg? Probably, but it would be slow and very hard.

At last I decided to take a light and walk up as far as the top of the mountain where I could yell farther. Halfway up I heard Joe answer one of my yells, and shortly we met on the trail. Not only had he come almost all the way back in the dark, he was carrying the caribou head and cape on his back. It had to weigh fifty pounds. I would have been proud to carry it the rest of the way back for him, but he refused. That's the kind of man who will fly the space shuttle. Not a bad choice.

The final day of the hunt came and I still had bagged nothing besides rabbits and ptarmigan, but the caribou were coming. We had seen them, so I took a blind at the first salt lick they would come to in our valley. I got there early and hunched down waiting for the winter sun to warm me up. No caribou were in sight. I read a book and got cold.

Suddenly I heard a noise, and there passing right in front of the blind was a caribou, then another, and then dozens. As they saw the lick they began to run for it. Some nearly jumped over the blind in passing. It was exciting. Soon there must have been fifty or more right in front of me. Nothing I did seemed to make the slightest difference to them. But I couldn't see one I wanted to shoot.

And so it went all day—caribou around all the time but either out of range or nothing I wanted. At last one magnificent head came in the far end of the lick. He was at least 120 yards away. Too far. But he was wandering around and might come closer. He was obviously hanging out with a smaller bull. Wherever one went the other followed. The range got down to ninety yards, then eighty. I wanted no more than forty-five yards. But now they had been in the lick quite awhile and were showing signs of leaving. Soon the smaller bull walked out in the grass going away on the far side. This was it, I knew. I stood up and estimated the angle. Not a caribou made an effort to run. Some looked at me casually. Finally I let go. It was hopeless from the start. A bow will shoot eighty yards and more, but who can aim at that distance? The arrow dug into the mud far short of the mark and my bull loped away.

For a long time no more animals came into the lick. Then late in the day a smallish bull with a few cows and calves came by. As the fate of hunters will have it, I easily shot the bull dead.

Back at camp we had an early dinner, and because I hated to quit I talked Joe and Fred into one last rabbit hunt along the runway of the landing strip. It was a pleasant place to hunt, not more than a couple of hundred yards from camp, and there were always plenty of snowshoes, which are excellent to eat. We bagged a few and laid them along the edge of the strip where they would be easy to find. I even shot a ptarmigan. But finally it was time to quit. Fred wanted to go back to the cabin, and so Joe and I offered to walk back the length of the strip to pick up a rabbit he had left there.

With all the rabbits collected, we started back, taking long shots down the runway, picking up our arrows and shooting again. It was just as we were picking up our rabbit arrows that we heard a grunt in the willows right beside us. Because I couldn't believe my ears, I asked what had to be the stupid question of the year.

"What was that?"

"A moose," Joe replied. "Shoot him."

Luckily I had left my big-game arrows in my bow quiver. Dropping my rabbit arrow, I switched to a broadhead and slipped to the edge of the willows. There broadside was a big bull moose looking at me. A barn couldn't have looked bigger,

and I had been shooting rabbits at the same distance. But I just couldn't believe he was so close, and instead of aiming with the same sight I had been using on rabbits I chose one for greater distance and let go. As far as I know that arrow is still circling the earth because it passed high over the moose and was still on its way when I saw it last.

"Did you hit him?" Joe whispered.

"No."

Groan.

The moose now decided to move a little farther along, parallel to the runway, still in the willows, and went out of sight. I backtracked into the runway and ran ahead to cut him off, again vowing not to make the same mistake twice.

Again the moose and I met, same as before, only this time I had my aiming figured out. Again I shot for just back of the shoulder. The arrow flew perfectly. There was a loud "bonk." It had stuck just in the edge of his antler, which covered his shoulder as the moose turned his head to face me.

As he tore through the brush I could see the arrow firmly attached to the antler, not bothering him in the least.

Back to the runway I raced, and fifty yards ahead again. This time when the moose stepped out I made a perfect shot. He went slightly farther on ahead and I thought I saw him go down, but the willows were thick and I wasn't sure. All was silence. In the meanwhile I had lost track of Joe.

Then I heard a whisper—a loud whisper—and I thought Joe said, "Come fast."

So out of the willows I raced again to the end of the runway and around the corner where the willows ended. The moose was there all right, and seeing me was all he needed to rise up and start to move out fast. I drew and hit him again right where I was supposed to. The bull charged full speed straight for the creek, and to my surprise right in his path on the rocky bar was our astronaut. Just when it looked as if a collision was inevitable—and I could see headlines, ASTRONAUT LAUNCHED BY MOOSE—Joe crouched in a ball and the moose stormed past, one antler passing over Joe's head. Thirty yards more and the bull collapsed dead, the biggest of the trip. Joe had actually whispered to me, "Hold fast," I learned later as we recounted the chaotic event.

And so what makes you remember one hunt more than another? If you have to ask, you haven't had one yet. But you will. You will!

A Critical Hunting Moment

ARCHIBALD RUTLEDGE

Any man who is a real hunter can remember with those thrills that time does not affect the really critical moments of his life in the lonely wildwoods, the snowy mountains, the sea-marshes, all of which have something about them that is primeval and changeless.

For many years I lived in Franklin County, Pennsylvania, a wild, mountainous, and beautiful country. In the great Cumberland Valley were quail and ringneck pheasants; in the mountains were grouse, deer, and turkeys, reestablished there by the splendidly intelligent work of the Pennsylvania Game Commission. As I knew something of deer and turkeys, I used sometimes to be invited to meet in Harrisburg with this fine commission. After the wild turkey had become practically extinct in Pennsylvania, the great birds for restocking were secured only a few miles from my Carolina home. The wild turkeys there are pure-blooded and very beautiful; moreover, such birds, *true* wild turkeys, have about them an artistic elegance that barnyard breeds totally lack. A real wild turkey seems always poised for swift escape, either by running or by flight; and the escape is beautiful for speed and grace.

From my mention of the wild turkey, it might naturally be supposed that I intend to tell of a critical moment with one of them. But I should like to tell of an incident more memorable. It has to do with what might have been a tragic experience with an old whitetail stag in the wild mountains of southern Pennsylvania. I then experienced my most critical moment; and you must judge whether I was a good hunter or not. Of course, as I see it, in every activity, including hunting, men have good days and bad days. No man God ever made is always at his best. At times his judgment and his coordination are sure to fail. Mine might have failed me this time.

When I lived in Pennsylvania I loved to hunt quail, grouse, and turkeys; but I went deer hunting only three or four times. This was, I think, because I lived in a small rural community; and when the deer season came on (and it was very short), men, women, and children took to the woods with high-powered rifles. Most of these hunters had never even seen a deer; and after a good many narrow escapes, I developed the suspicion that to my friends and neighbors I must have looked exactly like an old buck. Whenever a man begins to feel that he is a target, the chances are that his enthusiasm for hunting is going to wane. Whether I was ever actually shot at, I do not know; but so many bullets from fine rifles came my way that I gave up deer hunting in that particular region. But this was not before I had had the experience now related.

I had a good friend, Tyler Wyndham, a mail driver, who traversed four times a day the rather wild road that crossed the high mountain separating the Cumberland Valley from what was called the Big Cove. For some time prior to the opening of the deer season on December 1, this friend of mine said he had been seeing the great buck of which he now told me. He usually saw him on his first trip at daybreak.

"I'd like you to get him," he said. "I have not told anyone else about him. I nearly always see him on my early-morning trip, which is just about daylight. But no one would ever guess where that old boy hides out. You know that high rocky peak that they call the Devil's Chimney? Well, every time I've seen him, he has been making his way through those vines and rocks right to the very top of that chimney.

"You know that grouse and turkey hunters have been in the mountains a good deal during these past weeks; besides, you know that some of the boys hunt these big coveys of mountain quail. That old buck seems to know that the deer season is coming on, and he has picked himself a place where no one is going to hunt him. If you can figure a way to waylay him, you might get a shot. And, oh boy, what a rack that old rascal has!"

My mail-driver friend was not a hunter, but he was a keen observer. I knew well the country he was describing, and that strange high cairn of rocks. But who would ever think of an old buck couching himself in such a place? But as the hunting seasons pass, and a buck becomes wiser, he is most likely to be found where you least expect him to be. Once while shooting quail in short broomsedge, I started an old ten-point stag out of practically no cover at all. In fact, he had flattened himself so close to the ground that I could not see his body at all; but it was strange and startling to see his great horns, which he could not hide, warily moving as he tried to hide himself better.

My problem was just how to handle this mail driver's old master who had chosen so unlikely a place to hide out. The opening day was hardly a week off. This kind of hunt called for a little crafty scouting. Above all things, I must not let this old buck know beforehand that I was up to anything. If the place was really his hiding place, I knew he would be there from daybreak until dusk.

Driving up that lonely mountain road one afternoon, I parked about a quarter of a mile from the Devil's Chimney. I had brought some glasses with me, and I studied carefully that wild primeval tumble of rocks. How should I manage a situation like this? But at the time I had no idea of the critical moment that the mysterious future had in store for me. Any man who goes into the wilderness had better be fully prepared for surprises, and careful about what he never expects.

After I had studied the Devil's Chimney for a good while, considering the nature of the slopes and the possibility of negotiating them, I made my decision: long after the wily old buck had left the crafty security of his singular hideout, and long before his return, I would climb to the very top of the chimney. He could not wind me. Everything would be below me; and I would be afforded a superb view of whatever was approaching that peak. The real difficulty was in getting safely over those tumbled boulders, craggy reminders of some primeval upheaval.

On the first day of the open season, as I had an eight-mile drive, most of it up a steep and winding grade, I left home at three o'clock in the morning. As always, my wife—a real hunter's wife, however ungodly the hour—had given me a good breakfast and a loving sendoff. Although it was the first of December, it was not too cold, and there was no wind. As my eyes became accustomed to the darkness, the starlight revealed more and more of the landscape; and all this country, though wild, was well known to me.

When some distance below the Devil's Chimney, I parked my car off the shoulder of the mountain road. Dense darkness was all about me. On some of my preliminary trips I had discovered a conformation about the Devil's Chimney that seemed to give me a chance at my mail driver's buck. About a hundred yards away from the huge Devil's Chimney itself there was a second cone of rock, not quite so high, yet commanding a view of the loftier peak and all its approaches.

If, before daylight, I could reach the crest of the smaller peak, I just might see the old stag making his way toward the larger. These rocky eminences were not bare. Out of the leaf-mold between the tumbled boulders grew honeysuckle, ferns, wild azaleas, and beds of grasses. On one of my preliminary trips there, with the aid of a fine flashlight, I found in the rich black soil some tracks of the old buck, and in some of the growths of thick grass I felt sure that I had found several beds.

The place this wily old boy had chosen for his hideout began to appear more and more wise and strategic the more I studied it. While the hunters were ranging the lower ridges and the benches where they usually found their bucks, this special stag had found and chosen a special place. From where he lay high up on the Devil's Chimney, he could see far over into Path Valley and into the Big Cove, could take in vast reaches of the vast Cumberland Valley, and, on clear days, could see Sideling Hill and, far off, the great Tonoloway Mountain near Hancock, Maryland. I could not but admire his strategy. He invested that craggy peak with wild wisdom, and with the mystery of the primeval.

Because it was a still December morning, I had no fear of certain denizens of the Devil's Chimney and its environs, creatures for which that immediate region is, in the warmer weather, notorious. Amid this wild and tumbled heap of huge boulders was one of the greatest dens of rattlesnakes and copperheads in southern Pennsylvania. But at the time I made my climb in the night, I could put all serpents out of my mind. The only real dangers I encountered were falls amid those mossy tumultous rocks.

With my dim little flashlight I made my way onward and upward. My rifle was a .250 Savage, with which I have killed a good many bucks; if it has a fault, it is that its speed is so terrific that a bullet is easily deflected. A twig will throw it off course.

I believe I got to the place where I wanted to be about an hour before daylight. The stars were glorious. Far away in the valleys on either side of the ridge I could see the lights beginning to come on in lonely farmhouses. I knew that hunters were up and moving, with their proud and hopeful wives getting them off to a good start. Some hunters are college graduates, some barely literate, but all hunters have something, and it is a privilege for me or any man to belong to this rugged fraternity, all lovers of the wilds, and stalkers of the wary denizens of the shaggy mountains.

After a little while I could hear the stealthy movements of creatures on all sides about me—those returning from a night's foraging, and those setting forth in the dim daylight "to seek their meat from God." A hunter who is in the wilds just before daylight or just after twilight will hear things he will never hear at any other times.

The stars were fading now, and dim daylight was coming. I

had heard some distance away three rifle shots, which showed that some of the boys were starting the season too early.

From my perch on the smaller of the two cairns, I was within easy rifle-shot of the road. I doubted, however, if anyone could make me out on my high lofty perch. In its way, it was as odd a hiding place as the one the old stag had chosen for his safety.

It was a misty morning. The fog seemed to be rising all along the ridges. My heart jumped when I heard footstep on the road between me and the tall Devil's Chimney. But it is easy to distinguish the footsteps of a man and those of an old buck. The latter shuffles along on his four feet. However, from long years in the woods I have found that the walking of a man and that of a wild gobbler are nearly identical. Nor is this unnatural, for each has two feet, and steps about the same length. In fact, I believe the only wild creature that a man might mistake for another man is a wild gobbler. The sound I had heard was neither of these.

Of course, I mean when the deer and the turkey are walking in leaves. On a sandy mountain road, strewn with rocks, a man may stumble and fall, whereas a turkey may hardly make a sound.

As the first faint blush of day began to come, a few cars passed me, and I knew that the boys were on their way for their first day's hunt. I wished them well; and I wondered what they would think of me perched upon that tall heap of rock in the darkness, awaiting my chance of chances. If the regal old stag made for his customary abode, I was a little afraid that the unwonted number of cars would turn him. But I took some comfort in remembering what an old Negro huntsman once said to me: "An ole buck—he gwine where he gwine." As with age a deer develops in wariness, there are one or two places for which he will make when startled; and he is almost sure to head at last for his original sanctuary.

At the time of this hunt, the Pennsylvania law allowed shooting to begin at daylight, which was generally taken to mean the time when a hunter could see clearly enough to recognize without doubt the nature of the game on which he had laid his sights. And it was now possible for me to recognize a buck if I saw one—or was it? For a good while no cars had passed. Far

away I heard a few rifles crack. Then, quite near me, in the road, passing my high stand, and heading for the Devil's Chimney, I heard one or two small rocks roll. Could they have been dislodged by my stag's clicking hoofs? I clearly remember how I clasped and unclasped my chilled hands so that I could handle my rifle as a rifle should be handled. Slowly I raised it as I saw a dim object come into view. I laid the bead dead on it. I saw he would have to go about thirty yards before he would be lost to sight in the wild tangle of green briars, grapevines, and honeysuckle that smothered the shaggy boulders. I would let him go slowly up the mountain road for almost twenty yards. By then the day would be brighter, and my shot more certain. At that time of the day, even two or three minutes more daylight may mark the difference between a hit and a miss. As yet I had not seen any antlers, but when an old buck is sneaking along, he often walks with his head down; if alarmed, he will throw it up.

I had marked a chestnut oak where I intended to take my chance, and to me it seemed a perfect chance. The edges of the road by the oak were free of brambles and bushes. The wind was blowing from the buck to me, and the moving breeze was little more than a frosty air. The distance seemed to me about forty yards—just right.

I have heard hunters tell of killing bucks on the full run in the woods at 150 and even 200 yards. I do not say it is impossible; but if it is not a miracle, it ought to be one. Judgment of distance in the woods or on the plains, and the capacity of a rifle to handle game at that distance, are among the most critical lessons all hunters should learn.

Now, high in that mountain dimness, my great quarry, that according to Tyler Wyndham's description carried record horns, neared the huge chestnut oak, the naked and noble architecture of which stood massively against the brightening morning sky. My chance had come!

My finger was actually tightening on the trigger, I believe, when my game came into sight, and I was ready for action. But instead of a great stag stealing up toward his daytime "nest," it was a man! My God, I had almost killed a man! Moreover, he was one of my best friends, for I recognized the voice of Tyler Wyndham, my mail driver, calling softly, "Arch, be you hereabout?"

Shivering more with what might have happened to me than to him, I climbed down from my perch among the rocks, and soon was standing with him in the road.

"I seed your car standing off the road, and came up to look for you to tell you what had happened.

"I seed the old buck, too, with horns like a white-oak top. He was coming right up the road to you, but one of those early cars made him flare down that gulch there. But I bet he's right on top of the Devil's Chimney now."

As far as I am concerned, he can keep that misty mountain-top as his sanctuary. As I shook hands with Tyler, to thank him for "putting me on" to what might have been a great chance in sportsmanship, I believe he was a little surprised at the strange strength and heartiness of my grip.

A man with a gun or a rifle in his hands—how wary and how cautious he must always be!

How Not
to Get Eaten

WARREN PAGE

The plain and unvarnished truth—and I've always wanted to watch some guy brushing Valspar on a chunk of truth—is that charges by dangerous game animals are about 97.4 percent the bunk. Either they're not charges at all but merely territorial demonstrations, as when anything from a gorilla to a Uganda kob or even an elephant goes through an elaborately menacing pantomime to chase you off his turf; or they're accidental routes of escape, as when a pain-maddened grizzly, or for that matter a scared-stiff calf elk, happens to make the error of running straight over you toward what he thinks is freedom; or they're the ultimate defense that will under the right circumstances be put up by any animal *in extremis,* by a Norway rat or sow Cochin China as well as by a rhinoceros. Calling such activities charges is outright fibbing, or certainly a grave misunderstanding. Most big-game hunters are fibbers from way back, because in their tales accounts of charges by game are as common as charge accounts at Saks Fifth Avenue. One notable adventurer and raconteur, a fellow Weatherby Trophy winner, throughout years of magazine work found it impossible to write a story of his not inconsiderable feats without including at least one bloodcurdling charge. Even the field mice were capable of menacing gestures, it seemed. And I found that *very* hard to believe.

Of the 2.6 percent remaining—my figures may be slightly cockeyed but you get the idea—which could correctly be construed as real charges I suspect, nay, I stoutly maintain, that another 90 percent or so boil down to the hunter's own fault. He committed some damfoolishness or other.

The late Hardy Trefzger, whom I had the pleasure of knowing up in the Yakutat, once got himself thoroughly beat up, chewed, and spit out by a sow brown bear after he unthinkingly got just a shade close to the old girl's cub. The mayor of Ketchikan, they say, did the same thing and then tried to chase off the large lady bear with a shotgun. Like most politicians he was compounding an error. Four years ago my friend Art McGreevy and his professional hunter had to shoot an irate cow elephant just because they messed around too close to a nursery group. Their intentions were not murderous but photographic, but nobody had told the old cow that. The tales are endless—you can't expect to roust a young 'un, or even push the mother into thinking you're rousting her little Oscar, and not get a reaction from the female of any species that can even remotely be called dangerous.

By much the same token, you are asking for trouble if you move to swipe some large beast's lunch. Life in the wild being as direct as it is, with food for survival generally at a premium, interfering with an established chow line is not wise, not with creatures equipped to resent such interference with fang and claw. The likelihood and the depth of that resentment are probably dependent on the conditioning of the critter, and on the momentary need for food. A man-wise lion with a bellyful shifts off a carcass more readily than one that has been on short rations, obviously.

I recall fishing a section of Alaska's Copper River—which is not its true name because I'd never reveal the source of such fantastic rainbow action—and noting a heavy and well-established bear trail along the stream. Nothing unusual, since this particular creek would see a heavy but rather short-lived run of dog salmon, and brownies understandably cruised from one riffle to the next at that time. But without salmon in the river, the bruins probably weren't around, I figured—rainbows being poor prospects for a bear's fishing techniques.

Then I saw a very messy mound of torn-up sod and sticks on the bank, with a moose hoof nonchalantly sticking out one end. It smelled high as a balloon, and the bear droppings nearby were fresh. Obviously a brownie had either belted down a young moose or had located a natural kill and had appropriated it for his own use, burying for later meals what he couldn't bulge himself with the first day. Without waiting to ascertain his whereabouts or even his attitude—with no catchable fish in the river he had to care deeply for that mound of half-rotten moose-meat—I waded back out into midstream and stayed there. The handy little M600 carbine in .350 Remington slung over my back might have been protection enough, but who am I to deny, off-season, a bruin his tenderized moose ribs?

Andy Russell and I once happened on a similar refrigerator pile in the blowdowns under a British Columbia basin. We loitered near it, watching for the grizzly. Eventually we became aware, from an occasional growl and bush movement, that the bear was loitering too, waiting for us either to glom onto his meal or leave the area. Since we couldn't see him, and he had located us, and it was growing dark, and it was a long ride over a bad trail back to camp, and he might be a sow, and one thing and another, we bugged out and left him his smelly meat pile. Better to be discreet cowards than dead bear-wrasslers, we figured.

Then there's the common charge situation when the beast is wounded, or gets badly hit, by simple error on the part of the hunter. Or worse yet, by reason of misjudgment on the part of either him or his guide, or both.

On the latter point a sad case comes to mind. A professional

African hunter whom I had known for years was lugged into a hospital, badly beaten up by a big black *mbogo* or Cape buffalo, as the end result of a judgment error on his own part. He had permitted a lady client, apparently a gal of considerable ambitions but less than considerable marksmanship, to blast that buffalo from too great a range, on the order of 150 yards he later told me, with a double rifle. She belted the buffalo in the middle, it ran into the shrubbery and there ensued a considerable waltz-me-around therein, involving both him and another hunter. Before the buff passed on from the cumulative effect of many fat slugs my hunter-friend had been both hooked and scrunched. He even admitted to his original bad tactical guess.

Or there's the situation, quite possible in Africa, in which the pro lets his dude clobber one bull elephant in a situation such that the bull's buddy or askari bull—and there may be several—beats up the countryside, including the intrepid but wrongly placed humans, in the justifiable anger of which elephants seem peculiarly capable. Another boobery of tactics.

Few professionals make such bloopers, preferring, like airplane pilots, to be old rather than bold, but it does occur. One Zambia chap of my acquaintance used to treat the cats so casually, expose himself so deliberately, that hardly a season passed without his being sewn up and shot full of tetanus antitoxin after losing at least the first rounds of a hassle with a leopard.

The business of bad hits, which is a mechanical error on the hunter's part, I suppose, rather than a fault in hunting strategy, is undoubtedly the most common cause of those charges that really are charges. The lion hit too far back, the brownie hurt by too small a bullet, the leopard struck somewhere but not killed five minutes before dark, the buffalo shot seemingly well but not on the exact button, and so on and on. These happen all the time. In the vast majority of wounded-animal situations there is no charge as such because the animal never presses one. He simply runs away and hides. He can be followed up and dispatched. Or perhaps he passed away after a short interval. The gimmick in these is that you never know. Sometimes they do indeed charge.

The first lion I ever took, a large but typically not very whiskery gent from the Northern Frontier District of Kenya, on the shot dropped into grass that was tall enough to hide a whole regiment of lions. Full of bravery and ideas about the white man's burden, Tony Dyer and I pressed in after him. Within forty or fifty yards we found him, fortunately quite dead, at least thirty paces to one side of where we thought he should be. Had he not been dead, he could have taken either Tony or me before we could have swung a rifle muzzle onto him.

Rather more disastrous was the situation which confronted a friend who found a pride of lions breakfasting on the elephant he had dropped the day before. The bunch spooked instantly save for a ponderously maned male, a real trophy. But my friend's shot hit him way too far back and the gut wound permitted the lion to move off for at least a mile before they came up onto him. He charged out of a concealing clump of brush, and thoroughly chewed up both client and professional hunter before being shot off my badly injured friend, who luckily survived the subsequent miles back to camp and a flight into hospital the next day. The point here is not that the lion charged, or that he so badly mauled two armed men, both capable hunters, but that the whole affair derived from that first hit, badly placed.

The wrong rifle can bring about the same sort of understandable charge, with or without results fatal to the hunter. A classic lion story of recent years involves a well-known professional who was in a leopard blind with his client's lady, their only armament, since she was recoil-conscious, a .243. A curious lion approached, the professional hunter banged him in the middle with the light rifle, there was a pursuit, the lion was found by the professional and his male client around sundown, the lion charged, the client departed for Johannesburg, and the professional blasted at the lion, which promptly began eating on his foot. Ultimately, the recovered professional was relieved of his license, and properly so, since the use of too little armament on potentially dangerous game is unforgivable no matter what it causes.

There are admittedly some real honest-to-gosh charges without any apparent provocation. Rhino, for example, are just stupid enough to come barreling out of the brush at a noise they don't understand. In Mozambique we eliminated a bull buffalo that had the night before loitered in a brush clump, after having

watered at the river, alongside a path through the shambas or native farms. He hid there until morning, when a local black, with a friend alongside pushing a bicycle, was hit by that buffalo and reduced to a pile of bloody rags, the bicycle pusher for some reason remaining untouched. The buffalo had retreated into the same brush clump, from which it was driven out by us and shot. Under careful examination it proved to be a completely healthy young male. There was simply no reason for its fatal attack on the innocent native. Such things do happen, and when they do, they make the papers, since the completely unprovoked attack is likely to be a fatal one.

In a hunting career which over the last quarter-century has included some thirteen African trips and sixteen to Alaska, as well as several in Asia, and has therefore necessarily also involved direct contact with most of the earth's animals that can properly be called dangerous, I can honestly recall only four serious charges, where there could be no possible mistaking of the beast's intention. That makes for a small percentage indeed, considering the total of "dangerous" animals taken—something like nine elephant, significantly more brown and grizzly bears, five leopard of various sorts, four lion, some thirty buffalo as closely as I can recall, and so on.

I flatly refuse to count as a charge a Honduras jaguar's jumping out of a tree practically over my head, because from the cat's point of view that was the way out and he wanted out, away from the hounds. I see no point in trying to make a charge out of an incident in which a Peninsula brownie, abruptly roused from a nap, came barreling downhill apparently straight at me, only to pass a few paces away. Yet another bear, hit when he was above me in the alders, may conceivably have been charging when he likewise galloped downhill directly for me, to get his quietus only a coin-toss above where I stood. He might possibly have been in a real charge, but I somehow doubt it. A bull moose during the rut once came trotting up to me and refused to turn away until practically at arm's length. But that was no true charge. If anything, it was love.

One of four pressed-home attacks must also go into the doubtful column. That was an absurdity anyway. We had been hunting wild Asiatic boar—much like the Prussian boar of Central Europe but from one to two full sizes larger, with a peak weight in the five-hundred-pound class—in the marshes of Iraq. Operating from a *belem*—a high-prowed dugout—we flushed one very large pig off a little island, and eventually, and foolishly, I shot where I thought he should be, swimming through the papyrus. As a gout of water splashed up from the shot, which probably didn't even touch his pigship, the boar turned for us. In moments he was trying to clamber into the boat. Since the local sheik from whom we'd borrowed the *belem* had thoughtfully lined its bottom with rugs, and since there were already four humans in the craft anyway, there was hardly room for some four or five hundred pounds of muddy pig, so I stuck my rifle into his ear as his snout hooked over the gunwale, and yanked the trigger. If that pig meant to charge, he was hardly dignified about it.

No doubting the dead seriousness of other porkers encountered during the days in Iraq, however. In the course of reducing the rather considerable crop damage done to the Arab farms along the Tigris and the Euphrates by these long-snouted tuskers, in two days we collected twenty-six, all of which eventually found their way to a Basra freezer plant and so to the galley refrigerators of freighters in that port. Pigs being more than a trifle stupid, in those parts utterly unafraid of humans who are locally forbidden by religion to have dealings with them and were unequipped at that time with defensive firearms anyway, it could hardly be surprising that others of the local boar tribe made serious passes. One pair climbed a dike bank after me when I disturbed their snooze under a palm butt; and another did his darnedest to do me in while we were both in a dense thicket of camel thorn. I was on hands and knees in one of the tunnels the boar themselves had worn in the thorn when after a pause to survey the situation he came barreling around the bend at me, foaming, chomping his foot-long ivories, the hair on his head and withers standing in violent anger. I recall afterward—the tusks, silver mounted, are on my mantelpiece as this is typed— saying a little prayer of gratitude for the slugging power of the .375 Weatherby, an old-timer that has been with me on most of the tough-game contacts and is therefore a longtime friend. The 300-grain bullet, pointed rather than aimed, took out his spine right where the burly neck lifted into withers.

Provocation? Well, we had, with a mob of local Arabs, driven him into that camel-thorn tangle once, and since it was evident that my foolhardy invasion of his stronghold was not to sell him a newspaper, he had reason enough to fight.

I somehow doubt that anyone can hunt elephant for long without running into a serious charge situation. The fake charge or demonstration, of course, happens all the time. I recall one Tanzanian bull who finally got sick and tired of being photographed front, back, and sideways, and "charged" the car. But his trunk was out, his ears relaxed, and at about the time Tony got the Land Rover into first gear he had veered off anyway, having made his point. Most animals commonly make territorial demonstrations, even the essentially harmless ones. But ultimately elephant will press home their intent to kill or rid themselves of an intruder, with or without having been wounded beforehand.

In the Belgian Congo, just a few months before it blew up into open riot and rebellion, my Swiss friend Tommy Aman, a dealer in fine leathers and a frustrated would-be professional hunter, his chum an innkeeper from Ruanda, and I were hunting elephant on the Rutshuru Plain above the Lake Kivu area. Across this pie-shaped flat, thirty-odd miles long, the elephant shift between the Parc Albert to Queen Elizabeth Park on the Uganda side, and it's a fine place to watch for big ivory. On a local rumor that a sizable bit of jungle with a water hole in its center also hid a passel of large elephant, we had poked in there on the trail of one with super-sized feet.

The three of us, with two Congolese from the game department along for the ride, as it were, eventually worked in close enough to hear that belly-rumbling purr, the contentment sound elephant make when they're full and happy. A shift in wind made them turn that off, and two small cows shortly ran out, fifteen or twenty yards from us. Behind them came a huge elephant, tall as a house it seemed, but absolutely without ivory, and so apparently also a cow. She came to the fifteen-yard point and stopped, first unreeled a firehose trunk as if to make us out, then curled it again, hiked her ears, and as the two Congolese tried to disappear underground, came at us. Two steps was enough and three large-caliber slugs drove into the trunk top, just below eye level. No beast could have died quicker. Yet since it was seven steps from our footprints to the bluff of her forehead, it was hardly quick enough.

There wasn't any doubt about the charge—the Congo game

department, when we reported the incident, agreed it did not count on our licenses, was actually a case of *defense legitime*—but there could be doubt as to the old girl's reason. When the locals cleaned matters up and enlarged their meat supply, they discovered the cow had been pregnant, well along. That might account for her truculence, or perhaps she thought we were pickles.

Early on in my time of hunting buffalo with Tony Dyer, when he was still hunting professionally, we were involved in what the Britishers euphemistically call control work, on the upper cattle-raising areas of Mount Kenya. For "control" read "shooting in order to reduce a nuisance," buffalo having a habit of busting ranch fences, and of course grazing in direct competition to the landowner's cows. In any event, there were at that time no limits on private-lands buffalo. I had taken half a dozen when it occurred to me that these buff were not acting as represented. "Nothing to it," I complained to Tony. "One or two shots and they're down. What's all this tripe about the dangerous buffalo?" His reply was short and to the point: "Stick around." Since only weeks before he had been released from hospital with a massive goring wound in his thigh after a buffalo "do" involving an excitable client and a particularly tough bull, I figured he knew whereof he spoke.

And indeed he did, as several later events were to prove. Not all of them charges in the classic sense, perhaps, but surely tough fights between a man armed with a super-potent rifle and a buffalo armed with a ton of muscle, unshockable nerves, and a courageous determination to flatten any tormentors.

The buffalo is, I think, either the most dangerous or the next most dangerous of all African animals to hunt—unlike many EAPHA members, I've never so far run into trouble with the cats—for the simple reason that all of his faculties work, and work well. The elephant has superb ears and sense of smell, but poor eyesight. The rhino is much the same, besides being stupid to boot. Many bears have weak eyes. Most cats rely little on their scenting powers. The buff has excellent eyes, fine hearing, and the keen sense of smell common among all those creatures that are preyed upon. Further, he has an incredible ability to eat bullets, to soak up the impact and destruction of powder-driven lead.

The buffalo that had hospitalized Tony succumbed only after fourteen hits from thumb-sized slugs. Any professional can
list a dozen such instances of indestructibility. It is almost ax-
iomatic that if the first bullet does not hit precisely right to im-
mobilize the buff or spill his vitality almost instantly he turns to
hard rubber, and must thereafter be chopped down like a green
tree.

And among all dangerous game, in a fashion quite similar
to the ambushing tricks of the leopard, the buffalo will button-
hook, turn off his trail and lie in wait for the tracking hunter, to
hit him from behind or the side.

On one hunt in what is now Tanzania, I had no true professional, was with a hunting-inclined veterinary who has since
died in a Nairobi car wreck. Even so, we collected a better bag,
all told, than did Dyer and his regular client on the expedition,
Bob Johnson. And I might add, we lived to tell the tale, though
there were moments when we couldn't be sure.

One cool dawn we spotted where buff had fed onto a grassy
plain, and we could track the dew marks back into a long jungle
strip. We left the vehicle and sneaked after them into the dense
greenery, cut up with the paths the black bulls had worn. A
Waliangulu tracker named Nguyo, paroled to Tony after serv-
ing out a poaching sentence, was in the lead. At a little stream
we located the buff; I drove a solid quartering into the shoulder
of the nearest, whose horns were clearly outsize; and as the
bunch turned and ran off both the veterinary-turned-hunter and
I let go into what we both thought was the already-hit bull. Seconds afterward we heard a crashing tumble, and soon came up
onto the dying buffalo. As the gunbearers and trackers and I began the job of clearing brush to make easier the caping and
butchering I checked over the recumbent form and counted
holes. One entrance and its exit were missing, so either we'd
missed one shot completely or there was another buff wounded
in the area.

A circular sweep showed the evidence. First the clear prints
of a single bull, then frothy lung blood, pumping out on both
sides. A bullet had gone through Buffalo No. 2 and we had
serious trouble.

My regular gunbearer flatly refused to follow the wounded
buff, and therefore was fired on the spot, and off I went with the

Waliangulu, Nguyo, to comply not only with the laws of the country, which demand the following up and dispatching of game considered dangerous, but also with the ethics of the situation, which demand utmost effort on *any* wounded animal. It was a slow course. The bull was moving strongly along one of the vine-grown trails, and as the boy tracked I had to maintain sharp watch in all directions for a lurking black hulk.

At a fork in the trail, where a secondary path came in from our left, Nguyo stopped, froze. By peering over his head up that secondary track I could see the wet-shiny black of a buffalo muzzle showing only feet away in the leaves. The bull, knowing we were trailing him, had buttonhooked, stood quiet. Had we stepped along the main track he would have hit us from behind and both of us would've become statistics.

At the time I had in hand a .460 Weatherby, a junior cannon. With its 8000 foot-pounds of bullet energy I shot the black bull up the left nostril. Recoil momentarily blanked out the buff's head, but all the energy should, I felt, have either dropped him on that spot or given him the world's greatest headache. Yet it was not until minutes later, when we were crossing a little glade or clearing seeking to cut around to his rear for another approach, that we saw the bull again, this time on his feet and already coming.

It is hard to believe that a .460 can actually be fired fast, but I doubt I ever emptied even a rimfire bolt gun any faster, and every 500-grain slug went into the buffalo. Yet it took one more, into the neck after he was down, as a quietus.

I suspect it has been this particular experience with the bulking black bovines that among all others remains sharp in my mind when the talk turns to moments of truth. If we accept Hemingway's idea that the pinnacle of experience is that instant when the matador is poised with his sword over the horns of a Spanish bull, awaiting the final charge, with death an imminent possibility for both man and bull, then there had to be at least two moments here, since I was looking at Death twice, really— once when the buffalo waited for us to turn the corner away from his hiding place, finally when he started his final charge from what had to be less than fifteen long steps.

The moment of truth under any definition must contain a strong element of raw emotion, it strikes me, whether it is the sense of awe a hunter feels high on a windswept sheep ridge, the sheer joy of living he has when the night wind is strong through the aspens but fire warmth brings comfort to his face, or even the primal sense of fear no one of us can deny when modern man confronts the death-intent beast. Man's armament then is less important than what's inside him. And knowledge of that, I suspect, is the truth all hunters seek.

The Loita Rogue

RUSSELL BARNETT AITKEN

Although my moment of truth happened a dozen years ago, in a fog-shrouded patch of African bush, the passage of time is not likely ever to dim its outline.

A decade or more had passed since I'd been on safari in Kenya when suddenly I'd gotten the itch again. Shooting *zuritos* in Italy's live-pigeon rings, I'd managed to book passage from Venice to Mombasa, via the Suez, on the Lloyd-Triestino flagship *Africa*.

Next thing I knew I was back in Nairobi with that old feeling boiling up inside me, sitting in the office of White Hunters Limited under the mounted head of the bongo which the late Bwana Cottar, a friend, had clobbered way back in the good old days.

"What I have in mind," I'd said, "is a short safari into the Masai District—a little action with buffalo and maybe a try for a big leopard."

The director of the firm had cased me for a moment with a pair of penetrating ice-blue eyes. "If it's action you want," he'd said finally, "I might be able to get you Dave Lunan. How would that be?"

I said it would be fine.

I'd never met Lunan but I'd heard plenty about him. Maybe you remember the opening sequence of the film King Solomon's Mines where a hunter lets a crusty bull elephant charge to within fifteen yards before dropping it flatter than a flounder? That was Lunan, acting as stand-in for the star. Or in another movie, Hemingway's *The Snows of Kilimanjaro,* a sensational rhino kill when the oncoming brute was stopped ten feet from the gun muzzle? That was Lunan, too.

There was something else I remembered from casual safari gossip. In a profession noted for its caution, Lunan was the one white hunter who always hoped that his client would bobble the shot at lion or leopard so that he, himself, could have the fun of going into the high grass after the wounded cat, a pastime about as harmless as playing handball with a live grenade. A safari with Lunan might be many things, but it wouldn't be dull.

I met him next morning, a shy soft-spoken chap tanned the color of a moosehide moccasin. He looked like Robert Mitchum, only better, and his 185 pounds were evenly distributed over a six-foot-one frame. The scars where he'd been clawed by a leopard a few years earlier hardly showed at all.

Two days later, when it came time to start out, we ran into trouble. The hunting block we had booked was now one big bog from heavy rains, which meant that we'd have to hunt a corner of the Loita Plains for a few days—or not hunt at all.

I wasn't wild about the idea. In the old days the Loita was simply something you crossed in order to reach proper hunting country in the Masai, and it had never been exactly crawling with record-book game.

Late that first afternoon we pitched camp in a grove of marulas not far from Maji Moto and then set off in the safari car to find some camp meat. Although we'd passed plenty of Tommy rams no farther away than forty or fifty yards, standing still as statues except for that crazy, wagging metronome tail, the one Lunan picked for me was a good 190 yards off and trotting.

The Tommy is a gazelle no bigger than an airedale and I recognized the old ploy.

I was a new client and Lunan didn't give a damn if I'd shot scimitar oryx, galloping, at 500 yards in the Wadi Hachim or tracked down skittish addax in the shifting sands of the Sahara. He couldn't care less that I'd bagged bongo and Lord Derby's eland in West Africa, the world's No. 1 waterbuck in the Transvaal or the No. 1 Western roan in Oubangui-Chari. All he wanted to know was whether or not I knew how to shoot a rifle—right here and right now—in his own backyard.

Shrugging my shoulders, I grabbed the .244 Holland & Holland from the rack, jumped off the near side as the car rolled on and eased a cartridge into the chamber.

The Tommy, still trotting, was holding a fairly straight course. Placing the pipper of the 4-power scope high on his shoulder, I took a deep breath, calculated the amount of drop and forward allowance and squeezed the trigger.

At the *whunk* of the bullet the little Thomson's gazelle flopped over like a cast-iron duck in a Coney Island shooting gallery. Lunan, sitting behind the wheel of the safari car and sucking on his pipe, nodded approval and we were in business.

Six o'clock next morning, the first real day of safari, found us jolting in and out of pigholes looking for game. It had rained hard during the night but most of the downpour had been blotted up on contact by the bone-dry ferric red earth. Heavy white clouds lay like cottonwool in the deep valleys, reminding me of a Scottish moor when a pea-soup *haar* descends into the glens. It made an eerie landscape in which the Hound of the Baskervilles would have looked a lot more at home than the zebras which crossed our path, biting and kicking each other en route.

Dave climbed out from behind the wheel, took a good look, and whistled sharply.

"He's a bloody big buff," he said, "and he won't have gone far. Would you care to spoor him up?"

I reached back of the seat in the old teak-bodied International to unclamp my pet .470 Rigby double express. "Look, chum," I said, "I haven't come eight thousand miles to play canasta. Let us go pay a call on Bwana *Mbogo.*"

A gentle swing of the lever opened the breech and the two cartridges, a solid and a soft-nose both fat as dill pickles, dropped into place with a comforting *clink.*

We started through the sopping waist-high grass in single file with the tracker Kasuria in the lead and then Lunan with me just behind and my gunbearer bringing up the rear empty-handed. He was empty-handed because my heavy artillery was slung snugly over my right shoulder, which is where I like it to be when I'm playing tag with Cape buffalo and other heavyweights.

The trail, which took us through dense thickets of whistling thorn and past clumps of vicious wait-a-bit, was so plain in the wet grass that a Cub Scout could have followed it easily. In our haste, not having to look for tracks, we almost stepped in a big platter of dung still steaming in the frosty air.

Lunan studied the pungent stuff. "He's not five minutes ahead of us," he grunted. "We'd best be on our toes."

Kasuria, scouting ahead, halted dead in his tracks and held up a brown palm in a gesture which means "STOP" in any language. The buffalo's trail led off through the grass sharply to our left, but the old devil had circled on his own track and was waiting in ambush in a clump directly ahead of us and not over twenty yards away. It was dark in that clump and I could see absolutely nothing that looked like *Mbogo.*

The Nandi shinnied up an acacia alongside the trail to get a better look. What he saw had him motioning excitedly toward the left side of the thicket. *"Mbogo!"* he hissed. *"M'kubwa sana."* ("Very big.")

Grabbing his binoculars, Lunan glassed the gloom. "He's a big one, all right," he whispered, "but I can only see his right horn."

He swung around to look me square in the eye. "The other horn may have a broken tip," he said. "Old bulls frequently do. We can leave quietly, if you like. Or we can make a noise and get him moving so that we can get a peek at the other horn. It's up to you, actually."

Over the years I'd been through this same routine with a dozen different hunters, a simple bald test to find out if you've got guts.

Back in Nairobi I'd said that I'd come for some action, so I slipped the safety catch off the Rigby. "I think," I said, "that we really ought to see the other horn."

He nodded and hurled an epithet into the thicket—in English.

Nothing happened.

Figuring it was my turn, I decided to try Swahili.

"Jambo, Mbogo," I bellowed. *"Habari gani?"* ("What's the news?")

The news was all bad.

Out of that thicket, looking big as a Greyhound bus in that eerie morning light, came the biggest, maddest, nastiest Cape buffalo I ever want to see, and his little bloodshot eyes were zeroed in on my bellybutton as he headed for me at the speed of a Tiger Tank.

By the time I'd weathered that first split-second of blind panic and paralysis he was less than fifteen yards away. By the time I'd slammed the heavy rifle toward my shoulder and aimed automatically between those baleful eyes he was less than ten yards off.

After forty years of practice in the field I expect that I can throw a gun to my shoulder as fast as anybody but I never got that one clear up. By the time it was abaft my deltoid I'd already yanked the trigger, because I knew beyond the shadow of a doubt that it was then or never.

As the gun roared an astonishing thing happened.

The 500-grain bullet, with most of its 5030 foot-pounds of muzzle energy still intact, smashed into the oncoming beast with the impact of a French 75. It pushed him back in the direction he'd come from, and through the haze of cordite fumes I watched in frozen fascination as the four legs with their massive hooves went flying up toward the sky, like a steer on a barbecue spit, and a ton of berserk buffalo came crashing to earth with a jolt that would have registered on a seismograph a mile away.

Stone dead, his bloody blunt muzzle was less than a foot from my left toe, and out of the corner of my eye I could see Lunan, his gun still mounted at his shoulder, looking like a hungry

dog who'd just had a juicy bone ripped out of his mouth. Behind me my gunbearer clapped his hands, roared with laughter and swatted me a mighty clout on the back.

More or less automatically I gave the buff my other bullet through the spine as Lunan walked over to study the neat round hole the bullet had made near the right eye.

"That was a bloody good shot," he said quietly, "and if I'd been behind you with a camera I could have snapped the greatest big-game shooting photograph ever made."

Wiping my brow, which was beaded with sweat although the morning was still chilly, I nodded. "And if you'd gotten it I'd have cheerfully paid a hundred quid for it."

I looked down with mixed feelings at the battle-scarred old rogue. An ancient bull, old as the hills, he'd probably been kicked out of his own herd by a younger bull. Undoubtedly he'd been wounded by spears or arrows or poachers' muzzleloaders and had learned to hate the world in general and mankind in particular. His thinning coat was almost bald, the boss of his horns worn almost smooth. He was plastered with mud from wallowing to build up a protective coating against the bites of the voracious camel flies, but the treatment had failed to dislodge the five dozen tortoiseshell ticks which covered his huge scrotum and made it look like a beaded bag.

Dave laid his rifle across the horns. "He'll go about forty-five inches," he said, "but bodywise he's far and away the biggest buff I've ever seen—a giant."

I nodded. "In Spain," I said, "when a bullfighter draws an oversize *toro* as an opponent he calls it a 'hippodrome.' I guess I've just shot myself an African hippodrome."

With the sound and the fury over, there was an intangible something about the encounter which rang a bell and it nagged at my subconscious all day long. It wasn't until late that night as I lay sleepless on my cot that it finally hit me.

Six or seven years earlier the editor of *True* magazine had phoned me one day. Fred Ludekens had just drawn for them a bang-up Cape buffalo cover for the mag, he explained, and did I possibly have a story in my files that might fit it?

I told him to send along a photostat and I'd see.

When it arrived I thought it was great. The hunter was in the foreground facing a charging buffalo in high grass at almost point-blank range. As luck would have it I'd returned only a few months earlier from a long safari in Northern Rhodesia. The patch of Sichifuru bush I'd hunted had been crawling with ill-tempered buff and I'd had to kill one which attacked without provocation. Although he'd been forty or fifty yards away when I'd clobbered him the situation was similar enough to cover the cover and so I wrote the piece.

What had finally rung a bell was the realization that the incident made it look like Fred Ludekens either had *déja vu* or a crystal ball. The fact remained that if Dave Lunan *had* been behind me with a camera to snap the split-second encounter the resulting photograph would have been virtually a facsimile of the *True* cover come to life, right down to composition, proximity to the buffalo, the high grass and even the old bush hat and khakis I was wearing. It sent a nameless chill creeping up my spine.

A couple of days later Lunan and I went on to our hunting block in the Masai, where I eventually collected an old tom leopard, wary as hell and only slightly smaller than a Brazilian jaguar.

I'd also stumbled onto a classic buffalo, an incredible bull with a wide helmet of boss rived like oak bark and a horn spread like the bumper on a ten-ton truck.

I'd stalked him in leisurely fashion and shot him undramatically from the middle of a herd in bright sunlight, and he was something to see as he lay there, black as coal against the emerald grass of the Masai. When we got the tape out he proved to be by all odds the best Cape buffalo I'd ever taken, the kind a bloke could seek for a lifetime and never come across—truly a trophy hunter's dream.

It was like striking gold and I was a happy guy.

But you know how it is.

Magnificent as this paragon of a buffalo was, the one I knew I'd always remember was that brave old devil who'd turned my adrenalin on like a faucet—my Loita rogue.

One Particular Dawn

KERMIT ROOSEVELT

For me, the "moment of truth" in hunting has come not once but many times, is not one instant but many, experienced in many and far separated places, yet fusing, as you live on, into one sum greater than the total of its parts. That is the always thrilling, generally chill, minute before dawn when you are setting forth upon the hunt. It is the tingling anticipation, the pretaste of excitement to come, the appreciation of the vastness and the unity of life that can overtake you as the world moves dramatically from the dark mysterious life of night to the bright, apparently more open, life of day. Whatever the quarry may be, jaguar or leopard, buffalo, tapir, canvasback or sandgrouse, impala or whitetail deer; or the place, the roaring majesty of the Nile at Murchison Falls, an icy duckblind on the Eastern Shore (the air so brittle with cold that you feel you could break your breath off inches from your mouth), or the steaming gray-green forests and marshes of Mato Grosso with the hounds already crying on the trail—whatever or wherever, this to me is the thrill, the essence and the irresistible call of hunting.

If I have to pick one particular dawn from the treasure bag—and it will be a pleasure—I will choose a June morning some years ago on the southern end of the Loita plain in Kenya.

The fire shivered in the black night, and the stars seemed to be shivering too. But the mug of tea Osmanli brought to my tent was steaming, and a breakfast of scrambled eggs and Tommy kidneys further fortified me. By four-thirty Kris Aschan—senior hunter with Ker & Downey, a dapper, rather dour Dane who had first hunted with Baron von Blixen, the famous "Blix," model for Hemingway's white hunter in *The Short Happy Life of Francis Macomber*—was checking our gear into his Land Rover— one .458 Winchester for me, one double-barreled Rigby for him—and we were off. Kris missed a turn in the ill-defined trail, so for a bumpy five minutes we plowed and plunged through dense, wiry leleshwa bush, noisy as a sizable herd of elephants, before coming out into the Loita plain, where we could pick up the track between Ngorengore and Maji Moto. The nocturnal animals were still up and about; a pair of jumping hares, like kangaroos with rabbit heads, eyes shining orange-red and bobbing oddly in our headlights, a porcupine hurrying to his burrow, jiggling and clattering like an agitated pincushion, and mongooses, sleek and low-slung with very long tails, which for some reason remind me of Sredni Vashtar, the feral, ferocious, demonic ferret of Saki's macabre story.

The light began to change, from pitch black to charcoal, then to oxford gray, then a greenish, smoky white. The night life was quieting, the yellow eyes reflected in man's light were fading, and the gray figures of the dawn, topi, Grant's gazelles, wildebeest, were emerging. As we approached our goal, twin water holes beyond Maji Moto, the eastern sky behind us was suffused in pink.

We left the Land Rover three-quarters of a mile from the first waterhole and, though there was not yet quite light enough to shoot by, began our cautious approach. We had been there the previous afternoon, guided thither by a Wandorobo we had acquired in lieu of the local Masai lion specialist who had failed to show up at the appointed hour in Ngorengore. So we went to visit a Wandorobo manyatta on the hill above. The Wandorobo, whose origin is obscure and much debated by those concerned with such matters, are in fact hunters for meat, unlike the Masai, who hunt only out of pride or to protect their herds and do not eat their kill. They therefore look down on the Wandorobo, many of whom may well be outcasts from their own tribe. There we recruited, or rather bore off willy-nilly for the rest of the week, a diminutive, fey little fellow who was said to be very knowledgeable of the whereabouts of game. These particular holes had water all year round, and there were abundant signs of buffalo. Our Wandorobo claimed there were two sets of them in the area, one a small herd with a large old bull which was actually watering in these holes, and another larger herd which visited regularly but watered elsewhere. The local people were anxious to drive the herds away, for they were destroying their crops.

Now, as we approached slowly, our pixielike friend in the lead, we could see plenty of fresh buffalo signs. Then there were sounds of an animal moving to our left and a beautiful bushbuck walked delicately through an opening some seventy yards off. We froze, but he took no notice of us. Beyond him we could hear heavier bodies and see movements of the foliage. Elephants moved past us on their way to the farther waterhole but close enough so that we could hear the rumbling of gas in their bellies. When all was quiet again we proceeded further, and were disappointed to find tracks of buffalo departing, over the tracks which recorded their arrival. Vervet monkeys and baboons greeted us noisily from the big fever trees before the hole, but no buffalo. The herd must have left well before dawn or we would have heard them. Reluctantly we concluded that they must be watering in the middle of the night, which would do us no good.

Without hope of buffalo but curious about the elephants, we went on to the next hole. As we approached, elephant noises, splashings and rumblings, the crackling of branches, became more and more recognizable. Our guide, having been told that we were not interested in shooting elephant, was quite disenchanted with the whole proceeding, but Kris and I were able to creep up to within about ten yards of the waterhole, where peering around the edge of a big rock, we found eight cow elephants, none with very good tusks, and a nursing calf, one of the most engaging beasts I have ever seen. I sensed a genuine affection between the members of the small herd, and also a playfulness as they sloshed water on each other and, somewhat ponderously, frolicked in the pool. I took some pictures with my Minox while the Wandorobo, twenty yards to our rear and well out of the elephants' sight, ostentatiously tested the wind with handfuls of dust. In twenty minutes the elephants withdrew, without having sensed our presence.

We also withdrew. There seemed no point in waiting by the waterhole; the Wandorobo believed that the buffalo lay up during the day in a heavily wooded, almost jungly area about two miles from the water. So, for an hour and a half, we scouted and searched through the forest. This was lively and exciting work, and our guide contributed considerably to the excitement, for he approached each dense patch of woods, or each turn in the narrow forest path, as if he knew for certain that a buffalo was about to come charging out. From time to time we would stop and listen intently, and often we could hear buffalo moving through the thickets ahead. The wind was very shifty, and when we finally got close to a small herd, they caught our scent and took off downwind. Kris believes that buffalo, and elephant as well, inherit a fear of the white man's scent. It is a fact that they react very quickly to the odor of nonindigenous hunters and do not seem concerned about the scent or presence of the local agricultural peoples.

We decided to have another crack at that same forest in the later afternoon, hoping that the buffalo might be coming out to graze as dusk approached and that we could come upon them before it was too dark to shoot. So once more I found myself trudging along behind our indefatigable little escort. His costume—a long strip of tattletale-gray cloth about two feet wide—was in constant motion, as though to guarantee equal exposure time to the various parts of his anatomy. I entertained myself by

visualizing possible routines for an exotic African striptease queen, Miss Wanda Robo, with her wandering fur stole—

You see it here, you see it there,
And all the rest you see is bare.

This kept me distracted for some time; I had to remind myself that, quite literally, a big buff might explode from the tangled greenery at any minute. But that did not happen. Time passed, and shooting time diminished. Then we were going through a clearing in the woods. The first three in line, Wandorobo, myself and Kris, saw nothing. But sharp-eyed Kipsoi, one of Kris's gunbearers, spotted the old bull on the edge of a thick clump of bushes, about thirty-five yards off. I had already given up hope, the light was fading rapidly, and at first I could not distinguish the shape of the beast against the murky, mottled background. Kris and I crept ten yards closer. The buff moved a bit, giving a fine shoulder shot. He was an old chap, with a good, heavy head. Kris nudged me and gestured forward. Shoot, he meant. I believe I was entirely calm and collected, but a slight misunderstanding with the safety of the .458 suggests that I might have been the least bit excited. Anyhow, having sorted things out with the safety, I aimed carefully, well up on the shoulder, and fired. A second later, taking no chances at twenty-five yards, Kris fired too. Both bullets hit on the shoulder, less than two inches apart. The buff stood stiffly for a moment, then fell to his knees and rolled over. I had not even noticed the seventy-two-pound "push" of the big Winchester.

With a shout of triumph, Kipsoi burst incautiously past me, eager to slice the old bull's throat and make his meat officially edible for the Moslems in our safari crew. Kris shook my hand with, for him, unusual vigor. "A fine head," he said. "Probably a mean-tempered old recluse. I'm sure we've done the world *and* him a service."

Even the Wandorobo gave an approving grin and a strangely delicate handshake.

A brief sense of anticlimax was soon overtaken by satisfaction. This was a good end to many days of hard hunting. It was a good end to a truly stupendous day's beginning. As I said earlier, the moment of truth for me was in that dawn, that and a hundred others, when the world turns from black to shining blue and you are part of it and all the great adventure that is going on around you.

The Lion's Share

BOB BRISTER

The sand was deep and the air was hot and still in the dense thornbush thicket at the edge of Botswana's Okavango Swamp. I was perspiring profusely, backtracking myself to the Land Rover after making some movies of our native trackers working the trail of a very large lion.

Suddenly the brush around me fell ominously silent and I looked down and felt sweat-dampened hair hackle on the back of my neck. Giant pugmarks had crossed my own tracks so recently that sand was still slowly sifting into one of them.

Perhaps some primitive warning had stopped me, and perhaps just in time. Botswana lions will take just so much midday pushing across the edge of the Kalahari desert. If the hot sand begins to bother the pads of their feet, they often double back into the shade and set up their own ambush. This one, I sensed, was very close and watching me. Now he knew who had been pushing him from one thicket to the next all morning. What he did not know was that the dark object in my hands was a camera, not a gun.

Mentally I cursed my own stupidity; professional hunter Doug Wright had warned me repeatedly about going around the brush without a rifle. But the big camera was heavy and difficult to operate with one hand, and I'd intended only to go a short distance from the Rover.

Slowly I began backing up the way I had come, then made a wide circle away from the lion, and when I finally heard the whining, brush-crunching noises of the Rover I got over to it in a hurry.

"He's right in there," I whispered, reaching for my .375 in the gun rack. "It's the same big track. He's doubled back."

Doug squinted into the searing Botswana sun, already starting its descent into afternoon, and shook his head, the excitement of the hunt draining out of him into weary resignation.

"He was there all right; you're lucky he didn't jump you. But he won't be there now with the noise of the car and all. He's decided to go back into the swamp, and there won't be enough daylight before he stops again. All we can do is try the palm islands tomorrow, because that's where he'll be."

We drove along slowly, following the tracks in the Rover and crashing through the brush, but the trail went on and on toward the heart of the swamps until the trackers gave up at dusk.

Doug Wright, as usual, had been right. Although he is a young man, still in his thirties, he knows his lions as few men have known them and lived to tell about it. As the son of a Scottish trader dealing with the wild river Bushmen and other tribes around the edges of the uninhabited Okavango Swamps (a South African wilderness larger than many U.S. states), Doug literally grew up hunting lions. As a teenager he hunted with older friends for sport. Later as an employee of the veterinary department of the British protectorate of what was then Bechuanaland, he hunted lions as vermin in the country's attempt to reduce depredations against native livestock around the edges of the swamp.

He was only sixteen when a big lioness doubled back on her trail, waited for him to come within a few steps, and made one of those split-second leaps and bounds which only the luckiest of well-placed shots can stop in time. His shot was not quite lucky enough. The momentum of her charge carried him to the ground, and only by throwing his elbow in front of his face was he able to stave off her dying lunges. She died mauling him, but Doug was almost dead, too, the elbow and arm still in her mouth crunched into a bloody mess. He never regained full use of that arm or hand, except perhaps when it grips the forestock of a rifle.

Less than a year later, with the arm still not completely healed, he shot a mauling lion off his brother. And he has stopped six lion charges since, all at very close range. He is the fastest, deadliest man with a .458 I have seen.

As we bounced along that night on the way back to camp I thought of the long scar on his arm and the fingers that can never be fully used again and I also thought of the sudden silence of that thornbush thicket and how lucky I had been, perhaps, to stop when I did.

The lions of the Okavango, I had already learned, are not at all like those I had hunted a few years earlier in Kenya. They were much larger, but the main difference was in attitude. Perhaps because of the lack of human habitation in the Okavango, they seemed almost scornful of man.

Only three days before we had driven up upon a big lioness stalking a wart hog. She had seen the Rover, glared balefully at us, and then continued her stalk not twenty-five yards from three humans in plain view of the vehicle. We'd heard the pig's agonized squeals in the brush, and I'd realized right then the true nature of those giant Botswana lions. Instead of being afraid of us, she had just seemed to resent the intrusion.

Lionel Palmer, co-owner of Safari South, with whom we were hunting, had been in on the kill of more lions than Doug Wright, because he was hunting them when Doug was a child.

That night around the fire the two of them swapped tales of lions that had charged, including no less than four (all lionesses) which had jumped at or upon Palmer's open Land Rover. The story they considered funniest was of a big female which jumped from thick brush onto the bonnet (hood) of the vehicle and rode there until Palmer could stop, drag his rifle out of the gun rack, and dispatch her as she snarled and clawed at the windshield. That story, by the way, was well confirmed by Palmer's native tracker, Big John, who now refuses to ride through the thick brush unless the boss has a rifle ready on the seat beside him. If Palmer forgets, John just bails out and waits until the mistake is rectified.

Sleep came slowly that night as I reviewed time and again Doug's emergency lion procedures, the most significant item being to shoot low. "They come so fast, man, you have to lead by shooting a little low. All that hair hackled up on top of his head is just empty space, and that makes you tend to shoot high to begin with. If he's coming, try and hold low on his chest, and don't wait, shoot and keep shooting."

That is apparently exactly what I was doing in my dreams when my wife shook me awake and suggested she would like to sleep some, too.

The sky was still red with dawn the next morning when Doug began grinding the Rover across the edge of the swamp, in the general direction the big lion had gone. It was an area we had not hunted before and I quickly saw why. By ten a.m. we had been stuck in the mud and shallow water twice.

October is dry season in the Okavango, with desert cool temperatures at night quickly rising to well over 100 degrees and the lip-chapping dryness of desert winds by midday. There are tens of thousands of acres of shallow water remaining from the wet season, which gradually evaporate into muddy ooze separated by high islands of dense and towering timber and small islands of palm.

It was just such a palm island Doug had said the big lion would head for, one of the larger ones covering several acres where the odds of seeing him would be poor unless we could find a fresh kill and track him again.

The odds of a fresh kill were good because huge herds of game concentrate around the islands in the swamp. They use the dense cover during the heat of the day and then feed on the lush new grass which sprouts up as the waters slowly recede. Cape buffalo are there in herds of thousands, tsessebe antelope, impala, zebra, wildebeest, baboons, wart hogs . . . a sort of living smorgasbord for a pride of lions lying in wait in the cool darkness of a palm island.

Doug said the big old male had separated from his pride when we got on his trail, but would now probably rejoin them in the palm islands. He explained that the unusual-looking clumps of palm surrounded by mud and water were in effect created by termite mounds which, as the land is piled higher by the insects, eventually become receptive to vegetation. The heart of each of the islands is thus a tall termite mound, an ideal vantage point for lions to lie in wait for some unsuspecting buffalo to come in out of the sun.

Despite all the other game handy, the most common prey of the giant Okavango lions is the Cape buffalo; of all the kills we saw during six weeks of hunting about three-fourths were buffalo, several of them mature bulls.

As Doug put it, even a big bull buff is "a piece of cake" for these lions which average well over nine feet. He said there are three lion subspecies in the concession areas hunted by Safari South, Ltd. One (and according to him usually the smallest in body size) is the so-called black mane, which at maturity acquires the dark mane so coveted by trophy hunters. The so-called desert subspecies, found mostly in the more arid edges of the Kalahari desert, has practically no mane at all but grows to very large size. Of equal size are the so-called honey mane lions, which are most commonly found in the dense palm island country. That is the sort of lion Doug believed we were after.

All morning we crisscrossed the palm islands, seeing game constantly but no fresh sign of lions. At noon we parked on a high termite mound in the shade of some palms and ate a few bites of canned salmon, swatted a few tsetse flies, and loaded back into the Rover.

Just as we rolled down the incline from the mound, my wife Sandy glanced over to a nearby island and asked Doug about some unusual "stumps" in the shade of a palm thicket.

Doug nearly came out of his seat. The first "stump" stood up, a big male lion with very little mane. Then another got up, then a big lioness. Suddenly lions were taking off loping across the marsh in all directions, and Doug was racing full speed ahead, dodging buffalo wallows.

Just as we pulled even with the island, maybe twenty yards

from it, the most magnificent creature I have ever seen slowly stood up, stretched, and arrogantly strode into the shadows of the dwarf palms.

Doug screeched the brakes and beat on the steering wheel in frustration. "My God, what a lion!" he groaned. "If we'd just seen him sooner!"

I asked about going in after him.

Doug held up his left arm, the crooked one with the long, deep scar on it. "Go in that palm island, Bwana," he said, "and that old boy will finish your lunch for you."

So we drove slowly around the island, checking to make sure the lion had not gone out the other side. He had not, and we knew he was in that little island of about half an acre, surrounded by a few yards of open marsh.

"He won't like being bottled up in that small place," Doug mused. "Eventually he'll take off to the big island over there."

On the theory that the lion would watch the Rover and then try and slip out through the tall marsh grass, Doug and I eased out of the vehicle and the head tracker, Wicket, drove it around to the other side while we hid in the grass.

It was hot in the sun, and the minutes dragged. Tsetse flies from the dark coolness of the island found us and began their buzzing bother. Although they had been no real problem in the moving vehicle, we were sitting ducks for them in the swamp and sometimes when they bite and touch a nerve they sting like fire.

After an hour Doug stood up scowling. "He knows we're here," he decided. "He'll just stay in there until dark unless maybe we can make him angry enough to come out. Sometimes old lions like that have been shot at, and sometimes they'll charge if a shot is fired anywhere near 'em. I once had a lion we didn't know was anywhere around after the client shot an impala in some thicket."

"OK," I said. "You shoot into the thicket and I'll be ready."

"No." He smiled. "I've shot a lot more charging lions than you have. You shoot into the trees, get another shell in quick as you can work the bolt, and I'll stay ready with the .458."

A couple of birds fluttered out of the palms at the roar of my .375, but nothing else moved.

"If we just walked to the edge maybe he'd spook out of the other side or something," I argued.

Doug shook his head sadly at my innocence. "Right now he's probably lying on top of that termite mound in there watching us." He pondered. "He feels trapped in there, and if you got close enough he'd be all over you before you ever saw him. I know what I'm talking about; you just aren't going in there, period."

The Land Rover came gunning around the corner of the island, the trackers and my wife wide-eyed because they'd heard the single shot and thought apparently either the worst or best. Doug waved them back around to the other side of the island, to make sure the lion didn't sneak out.

We could hear the hunting car grinding around through the mud and water, and suddenly the palms rustled and we saw a tawny flash of movement at the entrance of the largest game trail.

A guttural, warning growl echoed in the stillness of the island.

"He's had about enough of this," Doug whispered. "If you fire again he may come."

One more time I checked the magazine of the old prewar Model 70 Winchester to make sure it was loaded to capacity, stuck an extra shell in my belt for an emergency, and looked to see if Doug was ready.

Instead of his usual cocky little smile, he was dead serious, .458 at ready, eyes riveted on the entrance of the game trail into the island.

The moment of truth had come.

I picked the top of a tall palm for an aiming point, making sure it was well away from the direction of the Rover, and squeezed the trigger. As the rifle bucked, I had the bolt started back and in that instant a huge, golden-maned lion stepped out of the palms and saw us just as the sights found him.

Incredibly the lion had become a low, blurring streak, and I fought the impulse to shoot at the biggest part and held low and fired. In that instant I knew it had not been low enough: he was moving faster than I had realized and he was staying low in the grass, just his head and mane above it.

But with the recoil I also heard the roar of the lion, and

there was a tremendous splashing and thrashing in the shallow water and grass.

"You're high, man," Doug was shouting. "Shoot again."

Then the big head of the lion was there again, closer, and I could see the wrinkles in his face and the wide-set dark eyes. The sights dropped between them, and that time with the recoil the lion simply disappeared. There was one low, rumbling growl which seemed to shake the wet ground under us, and then silence.

The Rover came roaring around the island, the trackers bailing out smiling and jabbering Situana, but Doug was still watching the tall grass, .458 ready.

Finally he turned, and there was a sparkle in his Scottish blue eyes.

"Do you know you just got one of the biggest lions I've seen in a lifetime?" he said with suppressed excitement.

We walked over slowly and cautiously, because sometimes there is more than one lion and also because "dead" lions have a tendency to come back alive.

When we got close enough to really see the size of him, Doug turned and shook my hand. "That first shot was high, just as I thought, but you were close enough to nick his spine and rob him of his rear end; that's what slowed him down. But he was still coming with his front legs when you got him here."

He bent down and picked up the massive head and the comparatively tiny hole of the .375 was almost squarely between the eyes, a fact I still attribute largely to a kindly intercession of providence.

It took three of us to drag him out of the marsh and water to higher ground for skinning and picture taking, and all I could do was look at the size of him and envision what he could have done to anyone, namely me, sufficiently stupid to enter his sanctuary in the palms. His forepaws were three times the size of my hand.

Doug produced a measuring tape and stretched it from teeth to tail. "Ten feet, one inch." He whistled softly to himself. "You know it only takes nine feet, six to make the record books."

I recall thinking that I didn't care if he made the record books or not, he was the most magnificent, ominously swift and powerful thing I'd ever seen. And I was glad nobody got hurt.

It took some time to skin him out carefully to protect the hide for mounting, and it was dark when we got within sight of the twinkling lights of camp.

Doug stopped the Rover and told Wicket to get out the .458.

"It's a little thing we do here; we just let the trackers each shoot one shot into the air so everybody in camp knows we got a lion. Silly, I guess, but the trackers love it and it's sort of a ritual if you don't mind. Also," he added with a wink, "it lets Lionel Palmer know to pour us a couple of glasses of Scotch to toast a record lion."

I didn't mind at all.

Black Cat

JOHN RHEA

The cable read, SIGHTING OF BLACK JAGUAR IN MINAS GERAIS BE-
LIEVED AUTHENTIC STOP TIME IS SHORT DUE TO RAINS STOP COME
QUICKLY AND BRING HOUNDS MACHADO.

The date was December 2, 1968, and I received the message
by telephone in Boise, having just flown in from the Idaho wilderness area where I'd been doing a little mule deer stalking.

Black Jaguar, the rare melanistic phase of this species, had
never been successfully hunted by any sportsman, and to take

one had been a longstanding dream of mine. In 1967 I had hunted the Mato Grosso area of Brazil with my friend Alberto Machado, an exciting exercise involving crawling into a cave after rather an aggressive spotted jaguar. During this hunt, Alberto and I spent many an hour discussing the black specimen and whether or not a specialized hunt such as this would have much chance of success. The cable, therefore, started the adrenalin flowing, and notwithstanding the fact that I had no business even considering such a caper, there seemed to be only one logical solution—to go!

The first problem seemed to be that of hounds, so from Boise I called a friend in Arizona and arranged to buy one black-and-tan and one walker that had been used for two seasons on cougar. He agreed to have them flown to me in New York in care of Pan American Airlines. Then it was back home to Virginia for a winter-to-summer shift of clothing and the interminable job of "hound visas." Ever approach a Brazilian Embassy official and ask for an import permit for two "lion dogs"? "Sir, for your visit it is easy, I have only to place this stamp in your passport, affix my signature and you become an honored guest in my country. But dogs. Nobody but nobody imports dogs to Brazil—our regulations do not cover."

Faced with this potentially disastrous situation and with two very fit hounds eating their heads off at a kennel in New York, I mounted a telephone campaign, calling anyone who would talk to me—airlines, travel agents, State Department. Whether it was to get me off their backs or because they couldn't stand hearing a grown man cry, the import papers were finally issued. My visa was only a stamp in the passport while the hounds required a twelve-page document complete with gold seals and red ribbons.

What a relief when I finally boarded Pan Am on a direct flight to Rio—hounds aboard! Discounting the overconsumption of martinis, the trip was uneventful and Alberto was on hand to meet the plane. Everything seemed to be going well until the hounds were unloaded, at which time I was told by a very harried customs official that my twelve-page document was "not in order." There followed a comic-opera episode of paper shuffling and arm waving as well as other types of negotiating. Finally at five o'clock in the afternoon, one happy hunter and two thoroughly disgusted hounds were released to their own devices.

Alberto's Jeep station wagon, loaded with hounds, food and camping gear, departed Rio at six p.m. for the long drive to Montes Claros where we were to meet up two days later. Alberto and I took the evening flight to Bello Horizonte, capital of the state of Minas Gerais, where we spent the night in a really excellent new hotel, the Normandy. Next morning at seven a.m. we caught the twice-weekly Varig flight to Montes Claros, which lies on the edge of a vast ranching community.

I was particularly impressed by the friendly, carefree attitude of the local residents, who made our two-day waiting period a real ball. The fact that I spoke no Portuguese made little difference since everybody talks with their hands anyway.

On Friday, December 15, our Jeep arrived along with the rains, which came about two weeks early. The rainy season in East Africa has nothing on this area—it came in sheets, and while our hunting area lay only about 120 miles to the west, getting there proved to be a real problem. In the first place, our station wagon was not four-wheel drive, and after the first sixty miles the roads could better be described as a cattle trail/creek combination. Having left Montes Claros at six a.m., we expected to reach our general area by noon. At six p.m., however, we were mired axle-deep still some fifteen miles from destination. A can of beans and some instant coffee was all we could manage to get at without entirely unloading in this quagmire, so we spent a hungry and uncomfortable night. The next morning, however, fate looked on us a bit more kindly as shortly after daylight a local resident with two very large oxen appeared and managed to drag us about a mile to some higher ground. Some three hours later, both ourselves and our vehicle, completely mud-spattered, arrived at the ranch headquarters from which the original sighting report had come. The ranch head man was amused at our appearance but made us welcome with our first hot meal in thirty-six hours. It was there that we met our guide-to-be, Hymund, who had done a bit of jaguar hunting and had actually sighted a black cat some weeks before. Here also we picked up two camp helpers and managed to rent one horse, one mule and a very unemotional burro. At Hymund's suggestion, we decided to camp on the highest ground we could find some seven miles north of ranch headquarters and managed to set up some semblance of a camp before dark.

The next morning Hymund came to me and stated that

while he knew all Americans were very rich indeed, it was puzzling to him why we had to import our bait. I didn't understand the comment until he explained that we were on the periphery of a very large jungle area and that jaguar preyed principally on dogs inhabiting the local family shacks around this periphery. For me this was a particularly shattering revelation. I had gone to considerable trouble and no little expense to import my fine lion dogs, and now it seemed that in this area they were suitable only for bait. Alberto was perhaps even more embarrassed than I, but since neither of us had hunted this area we were able, after some tears, to see the humor in the situation.

We had tried to fashion a hunting technique based on our experience in the Mato Grosso and had intended trying to bring the jaguar to bay with our lion dogs. In addition I had had some special miner's lights made up so we could investigate some of the caves without quite as much danger as we had encountered in Mato Grosso. Jaguar have a great penchant for lying up during the heat of the day in the cool dampness of a cave. Obviously we couldn't use the hounds to chase the jaguar, since they were far too valuable to lose without at least some chance of success. In addition, our cave-crawling plan was proved futile since with the early rains all the caves had filled with water; therefore, they were unused by jaguar. There were very few trails other than those used by game and cattle in this jungle area; and even though the ground was soft, actually ankle-deep in mud, we picked up very few tracks and even when we did, couldn't follow them for more than a short distance. Hymund suggested setting some traps, but frankly I just couldn't accept this as a hunting technique. Each day became wetter and more frustrating, particularly in view of the fact that we were not the only ones seeking high ground. As companions, we had both snakes and tarantulas. I remember waking about daylight one morning and looking out through the mosquito netting of my one-man tent to find my view obstructed in several areas by large orange teeth. I had never before examined the underside of a tarantula from the distance of a couple of feet so was really unprepared for that nauseating sight so early in the morning. There were seven of these monsters about half the size of a dinner plate clinging to my mosquito netting, I suppose in an attempt to find a dry spot. This is an experience I don't care to repeat, nor the exercise I went through in getting them off the

netting and into a state where they wouldn't bother anyone any more.

On December 19 we finally managed to buy a few head of goat, deciding that if we were to be successful then baiting was our only answer. This, of course, called for finding small clearings where tracks had been seen or likely crossing spots for the cats. In addition, machans had to be built since there was no way to know from which direction the jaguar would come, and being six or eight feet above the ground would prevent the cat from getting our wind. For the next five days we got little sleep and were completely drenched at practically all times. Even the sleeping bags had absorbed tremendous amounts of moisture and had become completely soaked. The days were spent in searching for sign and the nights huddled miserably in a machan. The rain was somewhat intermittent, but that was a mixed blessing, since when the rain stopped absolute hoards of extremely vicious mosquitoes would descend on us and they seemed to thrive on repellent. Happily, Alberto has a very fine sense of humor and at least most of the time we were able to laugh off our miseries.

For rifles we only had two Winchester .30/30 carbines, obviously with open sights—hardly a satisfactory weapon for night shooting. We did, however, manage to tape my three-cell flashlight to the side of a carbine, which gave enough light to see the sights and illuminate the target at a distance of perhaps twenty yards.

In checking my diary, I find the following entry dated December 25: "Teeming rain—mud, mildew and misery. No point in even trying to hunt. The enforced inactivity coupled with the depressing effect of the rain is driving us both nuts—extent of my celebration was exchanging greetings and having a drink with Alberto. Both of us have infected legs perhaps from insect bites but they are badly swollen and very uncomfortable."

The two lion hounds all the while were living an ineffectual but happy life—consuming vast amounts of food and being exercised daily on leash by one of our camp helpers.

Our major troubles had, of course, been occasioned by the torrential rains—all caves flooded and the jaguar movement patterns undoubtedly thrown into a cocked hat. Our own movement was also considerably restricted; even the horse and mule were often belly-deep in water. I don't recall what coverage the

U.S. papers gave the floods, but the Brazilian government declared this section of the country a disaster area. Just thirty kilometers to the north of us on the Rio Verde some three hundred people were drowned and numerous villages completely wiped out. We were in no great danger except perhaps for jungle rot, but our patience was wearing pretty thin.

We got our first break on December 30. First the rain stopped and then a very excited young boy rode into camp about noon stating that a black jaguar had stolen his dog the night before. It seemed that the lad was returning to his hut at dusk, being trailed by a cur at some twenty yards. Hearing a sharp yelp, he turned in time to see a jaguar seize his dog and bound off in the jungle. Under questioning, the boy appeared absolutely certain that the cat was black.

Much action ensued. It was about seven miles to where the cat was seen, so a speedy reconnaissance seemed to be in order. We pushed our mounts as fast as possible but still didn't arrive until about four o'clock. The scene was easy to read—two well-defined pug marks, a few drops of dried blood and a bit of hair. There was no question now of the jaguar's presence, so we searched very quickly for a small clearing with a tree suitable for a machan. Having found a likely spot nearby, we managed to put up an acceptable machan, well camouflaged, before total darkness. Now the question was whether to bait that night or, because of the noise that we had made, wait until the next night. Hymund wanted to bait that night with a dog which he said he could purchase from a small village about two miles away. Perhaps I'm too squeamish, but I just couldn't stomach using a dog as bait even though this apparently was the cat's major prey species. Finally a decision was reached to bait the following night and to use a pig, which we hoped would be noiser than the goats we had been using.

Hymund was dispatched to purchase a shoat and have it available the following afternoon. Alberto and I took the long ride back to camp, arriving sometime after midnight.

The following day was sunny, steaming and almost intolerably hot, so we lay about camp discussing our prospects. It was decided not to use Hymund in the machan as on two previous occasions I had sat on all-night vigils with him. Good companion as he was, Hymund simply couldn't sit still and couldn't keep awake for any extended period. The entire night, therefore, was spent in listening to his snoring or his continual scratching—neither action very conducive to bringing a jaguar to bait.

As the day wore on excitement rose rapidly, and I must have practiced mounting gun to shoulder, easing back the hammer and pressing the flashlight switch a hundred or more times. We arrived at the small clearing about four-thirty in the afternoon and tied out our bait, and I crawled into the machan about five-thirty. It was decided that I should sit alone this night, since the machan was rather small and I felt that I would have more freedom of movement when and if necessary.

For many reasons I have never really relished sitting all night over bait, although I had done so many times both here and in India. The problems are both physical and mental. In the first place, one must maintain absolute silence, as even the slightest movement on a silent night will likely betray one's presence to an alert predator. Secondly, one's eyes have a habit of playing many tricks as the shadows lengthen and night falls. I have found a back rest to be absolutely essential, and one's feet must be supported by some sort of brace and kept flat with legs uncrossed so as to allow for the best blood circulation possible. Even then muscles ache, the neck becomes stiff, and some sort of pain is always present. One must memorize the area where the bait is tied and with closed eyes be able to draw a mental picture of the entire setting.

Night came about seven o'clock, and I was plunged into the Stygian darkness of a moonless night. With darkness came the ever-present horde of hungry mosquitoes that seemed to be bent on taking what was left of my blood supply. At one point I remember wondering whether the humming noise wouldn't frighten even a jaguar away. As the night wore on and I became more and more uncomfortable, I glanced often at the illuminated dial on my wrist watch, which was on the underside of my wrist so that I would not have to move my arm to see it. It became nine o'clock, ten, eleven. Finally, at quarter to twelve I began to wonder just what kind of a nut I was. Fifteen minutes before midnight on New Year's Eve everybody in the world, it seemed to me, would be pouring champagne, getting ready for "Auld Lang Syne" and a toast to the new year, and I sat very uncomfortably in a tree in the middle of the jungle awaiting a black cat that might never appear. One has to be a little crazy.

Shortly after this mental exercise, however, things changed . . . the bait, which had been from time to time quite noisy, suddenly became still. The night breeze that had been rustling the leaves seemed to drop off to nothing and I could feel another presence although no sound could be heard. Gone was all thought of pain or of champagne; just heart-pounding excitement. I fixed my eyes on the spot where I knew the bait was and kept thinking, "This is it! This is it!" Finally there was a whooshing noise, one squeal from the bait and then complete silence. "Wait," I kept thinking, "wait, let him relax," as I counted slowly to twenty. Rifle mounted to shoulder now, hammer back, finger curled on trigger. The flashlight beam cut through the darkness and all I could see were two yellow-green orbs looking up at me from about forty feet. I fired instinctively at the eye and was momentarily blinded by the flash. It took me a second or two to adjust and even find what I had shot at. This was the first time that I had consciously thought "black," but there he was, slumped over the bait. The long hunt was over and I had my prize!

Every hunter, I suppose, has foolish moments, and this was mine. Without even a second's hesitation or thought for that matter, I jumped out of the tree and went directly to the cat. I had no way of knowing whether or not he was dead, of course, and thereby took a needless risk, but such was my excitement. The shot had gone true, however, and I released the flashlight from the rifle, examined my trophy carefully, and sat, I suppose smugly, touching him, having my first cigarette and recalling all the troubles we had been through. After a bit the excitement faded and I began to feel very itchy. Not realizing immediately the problem, I simply sat like Hymund and scratched, until suddenly I knew—ticks by the hundreds had left the cat and were transferring their affection to me. The remainder of the night passed with my building a fire, stripping off all my clothes and by flashlight picking ticks. At dawn Alberto and Hymund appeared and were somewhat amused to find one small fire, one beautiful black jaguar and one naked hunter still tick-picking.

I often wonder whether or not I would go through such an experience again. Most times I think not, but then I haven't had any cables from Brazil lately.

Cliff-Hanging Tiger

JACK O'CONNOR

I was eating breakfast when the assistant shikari with the bicycle came puffing up the stairs to tell us that at long last the big tiger had killed one of the baits. He had ridden about fifteen miles as fast as his skinny legs could pedal his rickety old bicycle, and he had traveled from the edge of the reed bed where he and the other shikari had decided the tiger was lying to the center of the northern India town of Kashipur, a place of about 50,000 people.

I was then on the last leg of my first tiger hunt in India, and this was undoubtedly the last chance I would have to go home with a tiger hide for a trophy and a tiger story for *Outdoor Life,* the magazine by which I was employed. On a number of occasions I have taken a good trophy on the last allotted day of a hunt, and many times I have sweated out the last hours as I wondered if I'd get a story out of the time and money I had invested. But getting this big Kashipur tiger caused me more sweat, worry, and downright anguish than any trophy I have ever taken. I had traveled at least 12,000 miles and had invested several thousand dollars and a lot of time. Right at the last moment the Red Gods of the hunt relented. My luck changed and the hunt wound up in a blaze of glory. I am sure the reason was that they had decided that I was a real sweet guy, a dear old man who was kind to his wife, paid his bills, and loved dogs and children. However, these close ones bother the hell out of me. They are bad for the heart!

On that hunt my companion was a character named Lee Sproul, who had made a nice bundle manufacturing lace in Rhode Island. He was in the clear and as happy as the cat who had eaten the rat, as about ten days before he had shot a tiger of medium size back in the foothills of the Himalayas, the country where the late Colonel Jim Corbett had hunted down and shot the man-eating tigers he wrote about so eloquently in *The Man Eaters of Kumaon.* But so far I had not scored, although I had had chances. I had only two days left to get a tiger.

All this took place in 1955 when tigers were still relatively plentiful in northern India near the Nepal border. We had had several kills, but we used elephants to beat the tigers out and had only three—not enough. At least three times the tigers slipped out of the beat past elephants and stops. One night a tiger came to a kill on which I was sitting with an Indian lad who knew no English.

Pictures of tiger hunts always show the tiger in full view on the kill and snarling at the hunter who is about to give him the business from the machan (the platform built in a tree). But this sneaky tiger had neither seen the pictures nor read the tiger-hunting scripts. The kill was on the edge of some brush. The tiger sneaked up behind the brush, hooked his claws into the kill, and pulled it toward him into the brush. The first warning my Indian lad and I had that the tiger had come was the crunching of bones as the tiger fed. The lad, Durga by name, had my six-cell flashlight, I my Winchester Model 70 .375 Magnum. I had told our outfitter to tell Durga that in case the tiger came to the kill to turn on the flashlight when I gave him two punches in the ribs with my elbow. I got into position, switched off the safety on the .375, and gave Durga a couple of punches. But alas when the light went on I could see nothing but brush. The crunching ceased.

What to do? A week or so before Durga and I had been out one night spotlighting the very plentiful spotted axis deer for the pot when we ran into a tiger. It was about fifty or sixty yards away and all I could see was a vague form that was half movement, half imagination in the high jungle grass. "Sheer! Chute!" Durga said. I knew that "Sheer" meant "tiger" in Hindi. I was armed with a light .270 and my ammunition was loaded with 130-grain bullets. I couldn't tell which end of the tiger was which and I had no desire to wound a tiger and get someone killed. I refused to "chute" and the tiger drifted off like a wraith.

Durga was disgusted. When we got back to the rest house where we were staying, he told the outfitter that although that Burra Sahib (the Old Man—me) was a pretty good shot who could lay a bullet right between the glittering eyes of a spot-lighted chital stag and who had once plucked a lumbering peacock out of the air with a 130-grain .270 bullet, he was actually a timid old bastard when the chips were down. He had shown me an easy shot at a tiger, he said, and I had chickened out.

I thought of this while the flashlight played on the brush. "Sheer, sheer! Chute, chute!" Durga whispered. I didn't want to chicken out again but I could see absolutely nothing of the tiger, concealed as he was behind the brush and camouflaged by his stripes. I assumed that Durga could see the tiger and also that he had enough sense to put the bright center portion of the beam on a vital spot. Putting the intersection of the crosswires in the Weaver K3 scope right in the middle of the bright spot, I sent a 300-grain Silvertip on its way. The tiger gave a startled grunting roar and took off like a runaway horse. I could hear him crash through the brush for about fifty yards. Then all was silence.

At dawn Durga and I clambered down the rope ladder to see what we could find out. We found some blood but it was dry and black. From its relationship to the tracks I suspected a flesh wound on the right side of the tiger. In India the ethical hunter

doesn't go off and leave a wounded tiger. There is too much chance of his killing some innocent passer-by. We took up the track.

The tiger went up the bed of the main stream near which we had made the kill. After about three miles he turned up a side canyon. We followed the occasional spots of black, dry blood on stones and an occasional track in sand between stones up the canyon. I was hot, hungry, tired, and bitterly thirsty; as India is full of germs I was afraid to drink from the creeks. I was carrying my .375 by the sling. I thought the tiger was far ahead.

Then I came around a little bend in the canyon and there he was. My bullet had just skinned him along the jaw without breaking it. He was lying with his sore jaw in cool damp sand by a little spring. Tiger and O'Connor were both startled. O'Connor unlimbered his .375. Tiger made a leap into the brush. It was a Mexican standoff. We could follow his progress by the barking of the para (hog deer) and the belling of the sambar (Indian deer as large as elk).

Sproul had got his tiger on a hasty drive where we both stood on the ground to await the cat. I was in one fork of a nullah (river bed), Sproul in the other. The tiger chose Sproul's fork. Other tigers approached baits at night but got suspicious and did not come to the kills. One day a tiger traveling like a bat out of hell in front of a drive came by Sproul's machan and he missed it.

In those days the tiger blocks in the forests were open two weeks and then closed two weeks. We ran out of time and I thought I had had it. We moved out of the tiger-haunted foothills down to the Terai, the swampy plain which in the old days was the scene of the great tiger drives that maharajas put on, in which fifty or more elephants often took part. Now this great game country is mostly drained, cleared, and dried and full of Indians instead of tigers and barasingha (swamp deer, also about as large as elk).

We moved to the rest house at Kashipur. I thought we were simply marking time. The first morning we rode out in the hunting car, a decrepit Jeep left in India by the American army after World War II. I was profoundly depressed. We rode through a rich-looking country of cane fields, wheat stubble, villages, little patches of jungle. Tigers here? Preposterous!

Our three shikar elephants had padded down from the foot-hills and were waiting for us. They were feeding out in a patch of jungle and their mahouts squatted in front of the little tent where they slept. About 300 yards away in an Indian village roosters crowed, hens cackled, and dogs howled. Tigers nearby? Don't be silly!

Mukerji the outfitter sensed by skepticism. "Let's walk down the road a bit," he said. "The mahouts say we'll see the pug marks of tigers." We did.

Not long after a worried farmer came in to say that we could do him a great personal favor if we'd come along with him and shoo an old tigress and two yearling tigers out of his cane field. The damned things persisted in growling at his laborers, he said, and they refused to work. We tried driving the cane with human beaters, but the cane was thick, the tigers were wise, and the beaters were timid. No luck. While we were beating I could hear kids shouting happily at play in a nearby village. When I got back to the United States with my photos and my memories I wrote a story about the hunt for *Outdoor Life.* A guy who had never been to India wrote the editor that my story about tigers being found at the edge of villages was the biggest bunch of poppycock he had ever read and that I should be fired forthwith.

Very quickly we found the tracks of a very large tiger that lived in the reeds and bush along the river. He was well known in the area. He lived on chital (the spotted axis deer), sambar, now and then a humpbacked sacred cow or bullock or water buffalo that the villagers grazed in the areas of jungle surrounding the river. Occasionally an early-rising farmer encountered the tiger headed for his lair in the reeds. Tiger and farmer always noted the other's presence politely. The tiger was a good tiger, and the villagers looked upon him with a certain fondness. Indian cattle raisers have a saying about their cattle—one for me and one for the tiger. But this and the other tigers in the area lived largely on game and probably didn't take more than one cow in three or four.

Now and then when thoughts of romance came to the big old tiger he wandered through the reeds, the jungle, and the cane fields roaring in hope some lady tiger would answer— Oooom, OooooM, OOOOOOM! There was a bush-league raja in the area. He was called, I believe, the Raja of Djinn. We had rented his three shikar elephants, old tuskless "Joeys" (females). All showed marks of tiger claws acquired on noble and almost legendary shikars when there was more grass and jungle in the Terai and more tigers than there were in 1955. His nibs the raja went out after the old tiger now and then, but he didn't have enough elephants to make a thorough drive and the tiger was old and smart. He had never got a shot at him.

Tigers—and indeed all of the big cats—have soft feet and like to walk on roads and paths. Every day we saw the old boy's big round pug marks on the soft dust of the roads. We bought a half-dozen water buffalo calves and tied them where he was apt to pass them. Time and time again we saw by his tracks that he had walked by them without even stopping to look.

But this day we had a chance. The shikaris had tracked the old tiger to a long narrow belt of reeds that ran along both sides of a deep nullah through which a sluggish stream wandered. Somewhere in there the old boy was snoozing off his gargantuan meal of buffalo meat.

So we headed for the site of the kill, probably a dozen people in that one rickety old Jeep, most clinging to it like flies on a sugar cube. We unloaded by a pool about a quarter of a mile from the spot where the tiger had killed. The day was hot and the whole crew drank out of the pool before several of them left to tie a charpoy (Indian string bed) in a tree so I could have a platform to shoot from. Then the mahouts brought their elephants down to the pool to give them their daily baths. While this was going on the elephants relieved themselves. One of the mahouts had some sort of a frightful eye infection, which I eventually cured with antibiotics. Pus from his eyes was actually running down his cheeks. After he had washed his elephant he cleaned his infected eyes in the water. Next came a half-dozen women from the village. They all got into the pool in their clothes and modestly bathed themselves while dressed. Then the Jeep came back from the rest house with our lunch, soda, ice, and a bottle of Indian whiskey. Our personal boy decided that the glasses had got a bit dusty so he went over to the pool and washed them. I took my snort right out of the bottle without either ice or water that day!

After lunch the outfitter announced that the drive was

about to start. The belt of reeds that ran along the nullah was from fifty to possibly eighty or ninety yards wide. The country on one side of the reeds was quite open and merged into stubble fields. The other side was covered with thick grass just high enough to cover the top of a large tiger's back, and in the grass was a scattering of trees about thirty feet high. Beyond the grass the trees and brush thickened into jungle. Chances were that if the tiger came out he would emerge on the grassy side where he would have concealment and could find refuge in the jungle. It was on this side that I sat with Mukerji in that rickety charpoy tied about fifteen feet above the ground. Sproul and my old pal Durga were in another tree about 150 yards down the nullah. A couple of hundred yards up the nullah the three elephants were waiting to begin the drive. The reeds were about as tall as the elephant's back.

The elephants had not traveled over fifty yards before they got jittery. Mukerji told me that the tiger was near. But the mahouts moved the elephants on and presently they calmed down. They went about a quarter of a mile past my machan, then turned and came back.

The head mahout, a surly fellow who always wore an old World War I U.S. army jacket on the theory that if a jacket kept cold out it should also keep heat out, announced that the tiger had gone. He and Mukerji had words. Mukerji ordered him to drive again and the mahout took out his frustration on his elephant. He belted the poor whimpering creature over the head with a heavy iron ankus. Thick hunks of hide that looked like watermelon pickle flew off and blood streamed down the elephant's head.

Mukerji was right. That smart old tiger had sneaked around behind the elephants on the first drive. But this time he came out. I first saw him bounding through the tall grass about 150 yards away. He headed straight for the jungle, but a big Sikh whom Mukerji, who had anticipated such a caper on the part of the tiger, had put in a tree as a "stop" shouted as the bounding tiger headed toward him. The tiger turned and ran broadside.

Because the grass was as high as the tiger's back I could see him only at the top of his bounds. I missed him the first two shots (and in doing so I became the first tiger hunter in the world who ever missed a tiger with both rifle and typewriter). Then I realized that as long as I shot at the tiger I was bound to miss him. I swung ahead of the tiger with the third shot, fired ahead of him into the grass where I hoped he would be when the bullet got there.

I heard the bullet plunk. The tiger turned and headed back to his nullah in the reeds. I could see the grass moving but I could not see the tiger. I fired three shots at the moving grass and did not hit the tiger with one of them. Then I heard the tiger's death cry—part wail, part roar, part lament.

"He's dead!" said Mukerji.

The tiger had tried to make it through the reeds, but he died as he went up the opposite bank of the nullah. He lay there black and gold, massive, enormous. The three elephants, each loaded with shikaris, mahouts, and stooges, gathered around.

We took the tiger back to the Jeep on an elephant, back to the rest house in the Jeep. We laid him on his side. I drove a peg at his nose and one at the end of the last joint in his tail. He measured nine feet nine inches that way. When the story I wrote for *Outdoor Life* came out about two dozen British and Indian tiger hunters wrote in that I had not done the measuring properly—that I should have laid him on his back, then pulled his head back as far as I could before I drove the peg in at the nose. Then I should have rolled the tiger away and measured on a straight line between the pegs. So measured, they wrote, the tiger should have gone about nine feet eleven inches. Incidentally, this tiger measured over the curves from tip of nose to the last joint of the tail measured either ten feet two inches or ten feet three inches. However, it is the peg-to-peg measurement that counts. The over-the-curves measurement on either a tiger or a lion runs from three to five inches greater than the between-pegs measurement.

Tigers are somewhat larger than African lions. I have shot one lion that measured nine feet seven inches over the curves and another that went nine feet six inches between pegs. In the last few years several lions measuring a bit over ten feet over the curves have been shot in Botswana. They would be about the size of the big tiger, larger than any lion I have ever shot. In

1965 my wife shot a very large and heavy male tiger that went nine feet five inches between pegs. A large tigress went nine feet even and another eight feet nine inches. The hide of my big tiger now measures ten feet seven inches. It was, of course, stretched in the process of mounting, and in addition the hide laid out flat except for the mounted head is longer than when it is wrapped around about 500 pounds of tiger meat.

I believe my wife and I are the only two Americans who have ever shot tigers in India and not returned with ten-footers. One chap shot a tiger which either went fifteen feet and weighed 1300 pounds or went thirteen feet and weighed 1500 pounds. I can't remember which. Another hunter told me his tiger measured ten feet six inches, but it must have shrunk, since you could put two hides the size of his under the hide of that old Kashipur tiger of mine.

I have known two maharajas, both gung-ho tiger hunters who have been in on the kill of hundreds of tigers. Both said that about one male Indian tiger in a hundred measures ten feet or a little over between pegs. The Englishman Mathews Brander, author of *The Wild Game of Central India* and for a score of years head of the national forests in central India, makes the same statement. Brander used to lay on tiger shoots for British royalty and nobility in the good old days and should know what he is talking about.

The night after I knocked off the big tiger, Sproul and Mukerji went out to sit up over a calling goat that had been tied up to bring in a leopard—or panther as he is known in India. The Raja of Djinn heard I had shot the tiger and came over to see the hide. Our trip was about over and we still had about six quarts of Indian whiskey so awful that it made Tennessee moonshine taste like Chivas Regal. I hated to pour it out and I didn't want to leave it with the shikaris or crew because I was afraid it would kill them. I decided that getting the raja and his entourage boiled would be a useful and possibly amusing project. Within an hour the members of the entourage were turning handsprings and bellowing ribald songs in Hindi and the raja had the floor covered with blood and dead tigers.

In 1965 when my wife and I were in Delhi after a tiger shoot in the Central Provinces I ran into an Indian sportsman

who was also a tiger hunter. "I have heard about you," he told
me. "You are the old American man who shot the big tiger near
Kashipur. The villagers there still show visitors where it happened!"

The Watch
Fob Ram

ANGUS CAMERON

I have an empty .300 Weatherby magnum cartridge case sitting all by itself on a shelf of a whatnot above my desk. It is kept shiny but not shiny enough to obliterate a scratchy legend on its side, scratchy because its two words were clumsily engraved on its curving surface with the spear blade of a yellow swell-end Case jackknife. It says "Dall Ram," and to me it says it all. I remember incising it there very clearly, even though I knew at the time that it memorialized an event that needed no memento.

That case cooled out in the chamber while I lay on the bare tundra turf above a saddle in the mountains at the headwaters of the Sagavanirtok River in Alaska watching two white rams nuzzle their late companion as he lay white and still on the gray-green turf far below me.

That moment was a very long time coming. It was twenty-nine hours after we had left our little cruiser tent eleven miles away. Later—I counted them going back—I found that it was also long in coming because of fifty-two wet and cold crossings of the meanders of the little mountain stream we had to follow to find these sheep. But it was years in coming to a hunter who had always dreamed of hunting the Dall ram. For me the white sheep was the pre-eminent North American trophy, and I suppose it had become that for me largely because of Charles Sheldon's two books, *The Wilderness of the Upper Yukon* and *The Wilderness of Denali*. Over the years I had read these books from cover to cover three times and had read individual passages in them at least a score more times, absorbing the adventures contained in Sheldon's plain, no-nonsense, but nonetheless evocative prose. Now I knew why sheep hunting had so absorbed that famous hunter who had climbed for rams almost a half-century before me.

After the shot, Bud Helmericks and I had lain there in the bright August sun and watched the curious antics of the two surviving rams. We had watched them in sheer amazement later, for they taught us something about sheep—or perhaps they taught us something only about these two sheep, for who knows when he can generalize about the habits of any animal. As Bud shouldered his tripod and camera to do what he later did—and I'll tell that too in good time—I lay there and glassed a dead ram and his two survivors. Sometime in the next half hour I got up and unrolled "Old Mangey," an ancient caribou parka I had used as a rifle rest, and shrugged it over my head to cut the chill wind that blew across the hogback summit. It was cold there in the Arctic sun, cold enough to make me realize I had got chilled with the sweat that wet me from head to foot. I sat down, opened the bolt of the Weatherby and extracted the empty. Hitching about to get at my pants pocket, I found my knife, opened the small blade and awkwardly scratched D-A-L-L R-A-M on the bright case, and put it in my shirt pocket. For the first time in twenty-nine hours I felt relaxed.

Three days before Bud and I had begun the search by topping out from the shale-strewn shore of the little blue lake far north of timber. As we stopped to rest on the crest of the second roll of several ridges we could see the bright silver of our Cessna far below us, rocking gently on its pontoons. Nearby on the shore the little tent gleamed white and clear-etched against the limited palette of gray-green caribou "moss" and faded low grasses. Back beyond the camp, a half-mile across the high valley, the same roll of low ridges marched in orderly procession to a summit miles away. On our side we could see only one more ridge above us, although we knew from having seen them from the air there rolled away a half-dozen more such parallel ascending ridges at the very least before we could expect to see in full view the high, jagged, snow-clad peaks rising in the distance—or, more importantly, before these bare tundra ridges would break out 3000 feet above in the rocky ledges that sheep require near their high alpine grazing pastures. Sheep love the high bare meadows and valleys, but they want rocky outcrops close by as a quick haven from the wolves.

As if that mountain fastness were fully bent on displaying its cast of characters for us, the facing ridge produced first motion, then a form, that I thought was a grizzly but proved to be a huge dog wolf trotting lazily down the slope. In a landscape offering nothing green much larger than dwarf pyrola or saxifrage, this great gray-brindle beast, now fully revealed in our spotting scope, slid to a sudden stop. He dropped his head between his outstretched front paws, and with an intentness that we could examine closely with the 30× scope he watched those two new objects in his domain, the white tent and silver ship far below. For ten long minutes we watched the wolf watch the alien objects down in the valley. Finally, he jumped to his feet, switched ends, and took off the way he had come as if the Devil himself were after him. Two hundred yards or so farther on, he stopped again, and looking back, examined the new things far below him. Then again he ran. During the time we watched him a band of some thirty to forty caribou cows and calves had fed over the ridge above us. The wolf ran right through this band, and the caribou, as if they knew he was not hunting, merely separated sufficiently to give him a few yards clearance. After he was over the skyline the caribou continued their placid grazing.

When we had flown into the previously set-up camp, we had seen that the last ridges east of the valley were full of sheep while those on the western side, where the receding parallel ridges did not break out at last into rocky ledges and slides, had no sheep at all. We were climbing toward the east, and I remember that I could not decide which was the more exciting—the beauty of the mountain fastness or the suspense involved in being, I hoped, at long last in close proximity to rams. Our climbing routine was to trudge upward a hundred climbing paces, then stop for a brief rest, just long enough to let the fatigue drain out of our legs. Helmericks was, as always, in excellent condition, and now after two months of hard work in the Arctic, I was too. (I found later when we went out that I had come down from 212 to 178 pounds in the Arctic summer and early fall.) I was in shape, yes, but my walking muscles needed work for such steep and lengthy climbing. As we made our way up the succession of rolls, we sometimes stopped to eat the tiny blueberries that blinked brightly in the low, two-to-three-inch-high "bushes." They were small, but exceedingly sweet.

Believing that each step brought me closer to rams, I made the long grueling climb with good heart and high spirits. The carrying sling of the .300 Weatherby began to tire the muscle between neck and shoulder—but thoughts of the rifle's deadly efficiency easily salved the ache. It was loaded with 150-grain bullets at 3400 to 3500 fps and was sighted in for 300 yards. I knew precisely where it printed at 100, 200 and 400 yards and had figured out my holds on the basis of its coming target's anatomy. I would hold for a heart shot up to 300 yards, getting the arteries and lungs or lungs alone at ranges half the distance; I would be right on at 300. If the range seemed beyond 300 I would simply hold for the high lung shot and expect to hit the heart area if the estimate was right. I didn't expect to shoot at anything over 350 (who could not get closer?), but if forced to take a shot estimated to be as much as 400 I would hold on the line of the withers. With the practice of years of rifle shooting, I was not worried—then—about making a kill when the chance was offered. Also I had no doubt that the chance *would* be offered.

It *is* true that hope springs eternal in the breasts of most sportsmen. What hunter has not had "sugarplum dreams" of sixty-inch caribou, a royal elk, or, as in this case, a forty-inch ram? As one climbs for rams, the suspense has ample chance to mount with you. There is the vast panorama of distant snow-covered peaks, intervening ridges, shoulders, cirques, benches, slides and knife-edged hogbacks where erosion on each slope has left the top only wide enough for a sheep trail running along the summit. And the sheep trails! As we looked at the ridges across the valley we could see the trails clearly worn in the lichens and low grasses, clean-cut lines etched along the tundra slopes by countless generations of sheep. The parallel ridges, each hidden from us at one time by its fellow in front, rose in frustrating succession. Just when the climber had judged that the ridge up whose steep, open sides he was trudging would this time surely top out, he was disappointed to see another rolling up beyond. We were now seeing game, however. Even though the caribou was not our quarry, it was exciting to see them all about us. The bands were chiefly cows and calves with only an occasional junior bull among them. We called such immature bulls "mama's boys."

Finally Bud, above me, waved an encouraging arm, a gesture I took to mean that this time we actually *had* topped out. It had been two and a half hours of steady climbing. When I had got within a hundred yards of the long ridge's summit I ran those last yards and got a laugh out of Bud, who remembered doing this to me three years before when I had despaired of ever topping out on a similar climb.

At first I did not see the sheep at all. What I did see was a vast ocean of snow-mantled peaks rising in chaotic splendor all about us. Sawtoothed, jumbled, a vast, frighteningly beautiful disarray of rocky fastnesses, unrelieved, of course, by any trees here north of timber. It was a stunning sight. Immediately beyond, rising from the deep, steep tundra-sided canyon that separated us, was a ridge parallel to ours whose summit broke out in rocky ledges from which little fingers of tallus reached down to where the slope again became alpine pasture. The ridge was a mile and a half away, and, wonder of wonders, a hundred yards or so below the rocks, the gray-green pasture was dotted with white spots. Sheep!

One could see that these dots were sheep with the naked eye, but were they rams? My glasses quickly told me what my eyes had suspected. They were ewes and lambs, twenty-two of them strung out at approximately the same altitude or level along the slope.

We had crawled to the ultimate summit of our ridge when the rocky outcrop summit of this opposing ridge came into view. Lying there with glass and spotting scope, we studied these animals of ultimate wildness. There on the very extreme northern limit of their range they lay, quietly chewing their cuds in the northern sunlight with its curious quality of making it seem always morning.

To the man lying flat on his stomach in the friendly brown-green grasses of a tundra summit, seeing wild sheep for the first time imparts an emotion of sheer unlikelihood. There they are in the binoculars, real and palpable at last; at the same time there is an unreality about them; or perhaps it's the hunter who seems unreal to himself. I simply could not take in the truth that I was there. The sheep were gleaming white with their thin yellowish horns; bright curved scimitars they seemed on the heads of the placid ewes. The slow off-center grind of their jaws as they chewed their cuds was a curious accent of motion to their utter stillness. As I lay there Bud said, "Beautiful, aren't they?" as if there could be no other response. And there could not be.

A lamb rose and jumped sideways, then ran a few steps and looked about. Then another did the same and joined his companion a few yards away. Soon a half-dozen now-activated lambs gamboled—there was no other word for it—on the steep slopes. Their frisking did not seem to affect their resting dams; they lay quietly, legs tucked up digesting their recent feed. We wriggled back out of view, then took up our search down the five-mile-long hogback, walking a full half-mile out of sight of the sheep before we climbed again to the thin-edge summit of our slope.

During that glorious day we saw, near and far, ninety-seven sheep. Once, across the deep canyon where it narrowed to six or seven hundred yards to the opposing slope, we saw under a wild outcrop of jagged rock a band of fourteen sheep, all ewes and lambs save for one junior ram. His half curl gave even such a mama's boy a certain impressiveness.

I was exultant every minute of that long climb in the sun, and though we never saw another ram, we did see a grand sight that compensated for our failure to find the ram range. Our long

ridge rose to a roundish pinnacle at its end. When we had climbed to the top of this knoll and crawled over its summit to a place where we could look below, we saw on a bench 150 yards away a band of twenty-one ewes and lambs. Unsuspecting—not a sheep looked upward during the hour we watched them—they grazed and rested alternately. Several times a lamb sought to nurse, and a few succeeded, but usually the ewes hooked or butted them away in determined weaning gestures. The time had come when the young sheep were to be put on their own by their impatient mothers.

As if to put a final climax on this wonderful day, there occurred an episode that mightily impressed the two hunters. Tiring at last of watching the domestic scene, we rose to go. Before doing so we glassed the ridge to our right that rose across a valley two miles away. The ridge was cut with many sheep trails and overlooked, as ours did, a meandering willow-choked stream far below in the valley flats. Down one of these zigzag trails came a lone ewe with her lamb. She picked her way daintily, sometimes nudging the lamb ahead of her, sometimes trotting to catch up with it. At last they came near the bottom and instantly broke into a fast run. Down they went into the willows, disappeared, reappeared on our side of the thicket, and, still running, made the ascent in a matter of minutes right to the bench below us where they joined the band. This long run, two miles as the eagle flies and three thousand feet up, was made without stopping, an astounding feat that earlier in the day had taken us a couple of hours or more. We knew that she had made the run through the bottoms because danger lurked in these valley crossings. The next day, when we followed this same valley, we found the disarticulated skeletons of five sheep that the wolves had caught and killed on just such a crossing as the ewe and lamb had safely made.

As we began the long trek and descent to our little tent in the valley we decided that tomorrow we would hike down that valley in search of rams. It was midnight by our watches when we crawled into our sleeping bags. It was only half dark in this Arctic season.

Our map showed that the wide flat valley in which our blue lake nestled stretched a half-mile to the south before it drained out in a narrow, quarter-mile-wide valley flat. The stream, rimmed with willows some eight feet high in the bottoms, wandered in a tight series of serpentine meanders for thirteen miles before it came out at right angles to a transecting canyon of another river floor. The little stream, a dozen yards wide at its widest, sometimes curved against steepish, open slopes on either side, sometimes nudged low benches that lay ten feet above where the valley floor had been before—eons before the little mountain stream had cut to its present floor.

After many cold, wet, thigh-deep crossings and much fighting of the willow tangles we climbed onto one of these open benches to lunch on some dried peach halves and to brew a pot of tea on a fire made from dry willow twigs.

As we climbed the muddy bank to the open flats of the wide bench above, we could see the open ridges on our flanks, the summits of which we had walked along the day before. Off to our front beyond and perhaps three miles away we could see an L-shaped ridge with a shallow, sloping open saddle. In that saddle were three white dots. Rams? Our glasses seemed to show the contours of rams, and the big scope, quickly set up on its tripod, revealed not only that they were rams, but mature rams.

Amazingly the high-powered scope showed something else: each of those rams, standing in a line facing us, looking us right in the eye. If the sheep of yesterday had astounded me, this sight filled me with a rolling emotion of wonder and something akin to fear. There they were, close by, when I thought of my years of yearning as I looked at similar scenes in books and, wondrously, in the paintings and etchings of Carl Rungius. Now, a few thousand miles away from those books and prints, here they were in the living and challenging flesh; to tell the truth they seemed for a hot moment of fearful revelation as far away now and as unattainable as if they had merely been one photographer's artistic rendition for luckier men who had seen and appreciated and recorded these scenes many times in their wide and enviable experience.

As Helmericks turned the scope back to me again he said with absolutely dismaying calm, *"Now* you'll have to *choose.* All three of those rams are shootable, but two of them will make a hard choice for you. Here, take another look—"

Breathlessly I refocused the big Cyclopean eye, and instantly I saw what he meant, for we had talked endlessly in less immediate circumstances of this very problem. The ram on the left, estimating me as I was him, had a neat, tight full curl and then some; the ram in the middle showed wide, elegantly flaring horns framing his face in a kind of casual, insolent beauty of curl and taper.

"They're not record-class," said Bud with a grin, "but they *are* respectable."

Respectable? They were gorgeous. I remembered Elmer Keith's sensible maxim: "A man ought always to be satisfied with one, good representative trophy."

"But, but, can we get to them? They've seen us." My question was both plaintive and fearful. I was slightly embarrassed at my boyish alarm.

"Sure," Bud said. "They've seen us, all right, but they're not worried—yet." That "yet" was ominous. I had shot a number of head of game over the years—perhaps more than most two-weeks-to-a-month hunters—but I had never shot a sheep and that "yet" bothered me.

"Let's finish our tea and peaches and then see." Again the calm of an experienced hunter.

I suppose I did eat my tough, wrinkled-dry peach slices and gulp the tea which we soon had steeped, but I am not sure; every so often, perhaps a dozen times, I looked again at the three rams. Sometimes they seemed eminently alert, sometimes relaxed. Once the ram with the tight curl lay down. Evidently they weren't alarmed unduly "yet."

"Now," said Bud at last, "let's see how we can get you a shot at them."

It was clear that we must cross the bench, a tough flat of bunchgrass where the footing was never predictable, and begin anew the long climb of ridge after parallel ridge until we reached the one connecting with the ridge that held the saddle.

"We'll try not to show ourselves again," Bud said, "and when we get to a summit that gives us a view of the saddle we'll crawl up to see if the rams have taken alarm."

We walked slowly across the bench, and when our course was about to take us out of sight of the rams we had a last look to see if we could still see the far-off white dots. They were still there and had not run off up the slope in accumulated alarm, but would they be there when we next took a look?

It was a full hour before we topped out to a strategic point where we often walked the narrow sheep trails as we worked back and forth along the ridges' flanks. Finally a ridge petered out toward the sheep. At its end we crawled to the summit and looked toward the saddle. The sheep had not moved—at least to all appearances—more than a hundred yards from where they'd been when we had last seen them from the flats. Wriggling back out of view, we cut back along another dusty trail and out of sight continued our arduous climb.

The prospect of a final stalk, the exhilarating air, sculptured and snow-capped scenery with bright-blue sky and white cumulus clouds continued to give me a second wind. I had long since shed Old Mangey and stowed it away in the pack sack. Honest sweat under the wool shirt trickled down belly and buttocks. I thought often about which one to take, then quickly put aside such choices in superstitious fear I'd hex the stalk.

Late in the afternoon we came to another lookout on a higher ridge, and once again wriggling to a view through the low grass at the summit and peering over in a cap-off low silhouette, we saw the rams. As we climbed we also had lessened the straight-line distance to the sheep, and now we could see them nicely at something less than a mile away with our 8× glasses.

The big, heavy-bodied rams were grazing placidly, each occasionally raising his head to gaze far out and down across the vast landscape.

"We should get within range within an hour." Bud's comment was as much to himself as to me. Again wriggling back out of sight, we circled around and then, out of view of the sheep, continued our climb. We were soon on the far side of the last ridge and were wondering tensely what kind of cover we'd find in the last phases of the stalk.

We need not have concerned ourselves with this.

As we peeked over our ridge, now level in altitude with the rams and a half-mile away, we suddenly became aware that our ridge did not connect at all with the high saddle! We gawked in dismay at a deep, yawning transverse canyon between us and the rams that dropped dizzingly to a bottom where a tiny brook ran down to the stream we'd left below us. The canyon's floor was level with the valley we had left behind and below us hours before.

I remember whispering "Jesus H. Cheerist." I am embarrassed now as I was not then at such a fatuously trite reaction. It was simply appalling, unbelievable, and above all, unfair. Bud, usually a cool one who faced practical problems as they came, was wholly dismayed. More, he was furious at this bad break, and the worst of it was that there was no way we could have anticipated the geological and physiographic phenomenon that put us in this plight. The rams were still there; to get to them we would have to go down and up again, for we could see far to our left that this deep transverse canyon ran back far into the mountains. It was too late to undertake this now.

Once the shock wore off we lay there and simply chuckled in hysterical frustration. Unless we wanted to make a dry camp, there was nothing to do but to return to our stream bottom, make a makeshift camp and hope that the sheep would not move during the night or leave the saddle before we could climb to them in the morning.

So down we went, our braking muscles aching with the effort. At last, after picking a route out of sight of the rams, we descended in the fading light. crossed the little brook where the deep canyon flowed into the valley and made our way to a beach where we could camp.

Loose stones were soon collected and built into a kind of reflector fireplace, tea was brewed, and the last dozen of our dried peaches were wolfed down before we lay down to a hot-and-cold camp—hot on the side nearest the fire, cold on the side away from it.

It was a fitful sleep, filled with half-dreamed hopes and numerous ministrations to the fire. I remember once rising to put more dried twigs on the dying embers and staring up through the high willows toward the summit, where, I hoped, the rams were spending a more comfortable night than we were. The worn and rubbed caribou parka felt good against the creeping cold of the half-light of the Arctic night. Once when Bud's turn at the fire aroused me from a half-sleep I saw long, cold fingers of light of the aurora flickering above the peeks to the north.

At four-thirty a.m. we arose, collected ourselves and our gear and, foregoing even a pot of tea, began our long climb. Was it a futile hope? Could we expect rams to stay in the area, or within sight or possible discovery, for sixteen hours?

The mountain was steep, its parallel ridges numerous. The low Arctic sun rose halfheartedly on a clear day with fleecy clouds floating above icy blue-white peaks. The tension in me mounted in spite of the pacifying ministrations of the glorious scenery. It was a strange mix of emotions that ebbed and flowed in me as we trudged up the open tundra slopes. Once ahead on a narrow bench we saw a lone cow caribou, her coat showing ragged patches of last winter's hair that had not been shed. Emaciated and lackluster she was, for her right hind leg had been broken below the hip and flapped uselessly as she made clumsy, painful effort to evade us.

"How she has survived beats me," said Bud. "I'd shoot her to save her from the wolves if it weren't for the noise. We'll put her out of her misery when we come back."

The long climb seemed less tortuous somehow in the hope and fears of that ascent. I thought of the two bigger rams and vacillated weakly between the flare and the tight curl, then put them out of mind.

"Hell, Bud," I said once as we rested after a particularly steep piece of scenery, "they may be ten miles away by now. What do you really think?"

"Sure, they may be, but I'll bet they're still there, or in any case haven't gone so far we can't find them."

"Well," I said, "I'll tell you something. I figure our chances for a shot at them are so small that I'd be willing to exchange mine for two cups of coffee and a half a dozen sugar doughnuts."

"Yeah," Bud said as we began our climb again, "two meals of peach slices aren't exactly filling, I'll admit. I'd settle for one doughnut."

About seven o'clock as we topped a high piece of ground we saw the great rocky cliffs that rose behind the saddle. There was no doubt about it: the saddle lay above us, perhaps 300 yards behind a little round knoll that broke off on its right side to a jumble of broken slabs. Helmericks headed for this, got there before I did and peered between the rocks. I stopped ten yards away, too excited to stand the suspense. Without looking back, Bud extended an arm behind his back and made the little "come on" gesture. I felt my heart thump solidly against my ribs but didn't move, even though I was sure Bud was looking at the rams. He made the beckoning gesture again, this time more insistently.

Stooping low, I moved up and exchanged places with him.

The little amphitheater—an ancient cirque, it was—had been formed by a bygone glacier. Almost in the center stood the three rams. The one with the flared horns turned his head toward us and scratched an ear with his hind hoof. He walked two or three steps ahead, then kept his hind feet stationary and took a couple more steps forward with his front feet. In this extended position he stretched mightily, then, with great dignity, collected himself and lay down. Tight-curl and the smaller ram continued to graze.

It was worth the years of waiting and the hours of hiking and climbing just to be there and see this stirring sight. Our knoll was slightly above them; I estimated that we were about 600 yards from the sheep, and Bud agreed.

We figured that if we went around to our left the curving side of the chocolate drop might put us 200 yards closer. We could see no way to get any closer than that. A short walk and a long crawl put me on the summit, that part of the little knob closest to the rams. I estimated the range at 450 yards. As I caught my breath Bud set up his movie camera and began to expose film. In a few seconds as I glassed the three rams Bud said, "I've got to reload the camera, but it won't take long."

I had exchanged the glasses for the rifle, and using the folded-up old parka as a rest, I looked at the big ram with the flared horns. At that moment I knew he was the one I wanted; I also knew that he was farther away than I wanted to shoot a ram. The horizontal crosshair on the 4× Bausch & Lomb seemed to cover half the animal from brisket to withers.

Finally Bud said, "Don't let the camera noise bother you— shoot any time. . . ."

The ram was lying down facing to my left and I had already noted the source of Bud's warning. He said, "Hold as far back as you can and still get his lungs. Have you noticed that when he turns his head our way his left horn covers his chest cavity? You don't want to nick a horn or break one." I surely didn't.

It's curious that I had no sense of nervousness as I placed the horizontal hair just at the line of his withers and squeezed off the shot. As the rifle jumped in recoil I heard the "phlup" of the hit, and when the scope dropped before my eye again it revealed the ram struggling to his feet.

My old journal written that night in the tent describes the scene: "I was so sure he was hard hit that I didn't even reload. As I watched him through the scope this is what I saw. First he wobbled about drunkenly and then stood still for a moment. Then he lifted his left front leg, bending it at the knee, and stamped it twice. He raised his big head far back over his withers, then sagged at the hindquarters . . . once more he struggled hard, got all four feet under him, but could not rise. He sank back again, turned his head over on his right horn and never made another effort to rise. . . ."

I watched him without speaking, and in my mind's eye, I watch him now. It is a sad moment, yet a familiar one to all hunters—a powerful emotional mix of regret and exultation.

The other two rams then took our attention and held it for the next three-quarters of an hour. As I continued to watch from the knob's summit, Bud skirted down the ridge edge, worked along the saddle, and crawled out to within 200 yards of the living rams. They had walked about nervously, approached the dead ram and peered intently at it, until it lay still, and then had themselves lain down. Bud kept advancing and photographing until at last he got within a hundred, then seventy yards, and finally, standing up in full view, he was so close that he took off the telephoto lens and replaced it. At times I could hear him "blatting" at the sheep, and once both of them advanced toward him a full twenty-five yards. Finally they turned and ran across the saddle and into the rocks. When Bud waved me on, I paced the gentle decline toward the dead ram.

When I came at last to the little rocky outcrop back of which the ram lay I had measured 400 paces. The beautiful ram lay another ten yards farther on. I have often wondered how much more closely I might have observed the three of them.

Why do I called this account of two days of high adventure "The Watch Fob Ram"? Well, the day before, on one occasion as we glassed the sheep, the big one with the flared horns had stood with his rump toward us. His equipment had reminded me of a couple of old-fashioned watch fobs. He was quite a ram—on both ends. I still have the head and horns; the mountain oysters were probably eaten by one of the golden eagles we saw circling the remains of the kill as we made our way back to the tent eleven miles away.

"You Must've Missed Him!"

GRITS GRESHAM

The last 300 yards were the worst. Not that the climbing was any tougher, because the terrain was actually easier to negotiate than had been the case for the past hour. It was just that during those last minutes, last yards, a hunter knows that he is approaching that moment of truth. So it was this time.

The nearer we came to the top of the ridge the more I slowed our pace. With hand on my chest I indicated to Joe that lowland lungs needed time to recover, but more than that was involved. As an experienced outfitter Joe Blackburn knew, of course, that I needed time to get my breath, and he had already geared our final climb to that requirement. He, as much as I, wanted me at maximum efficiency for the final trigger squeeze.

Apart from my physical considerations, my dawdling involved a mental thing. It gave me time to collect my thoughts, to endeavor to appreciate fully the time span which lay immediately before me, for such moments are precious to me, as they are to most hunters. With luck, the culmination of much planning, many dreams, enough frustrations, and substantial physical effort was at hand. In minutes it could all be over.

"There is always the chance," I thought, stopping to consider the few yards which remained to the ridge crest, "that the ram is gone." It wouldn't be the first time—or the second—that the cupboard had been bare. In the past week that was exactly what had happened to me and Joe, on two occasions. And we had had three rams dead to rights the first time, and two the next time around. But they were gone! Vanished! Evaporated into that thin Idaho air as completely as if the mountain had swallowed them whole.

From a prone position on the crest Joe looked back down at me and nodded. The bighorn was still there, and when I eased into position alongside the outfitter and brought the binoculars into play, I saw that the ram had not moved. He was still bedded down across the canyon, just below the rim of the next ridge, exactly where he had been when we had dropped down into the canyon an hour and a half earlier.

The 10×40s snatched the ram up close in the eyepieces, giving me a much better view than had been possible even with the spotting scope from farther away. Haze and mirage played less of a role now, and we could evaluate the horns quite precisely.

"Left one is broomed off quite a bit," Joe murmured. "He won't make the book, but he's legal and then some."

As must always be the case, he was leaving it up to me. Do you shoot this one, or pass it up and look for something better? Two days yet remained in the season. Draw two more cards, or play with what you have?

A big-game guide can make most of the decisions for his client. He can program the hunt as to time to depart and how to proceed. He says when to tie the horses and go it on foot, and how to make the final stalk. He can give you, if he is a good guide, an excellent estimate of the quality of a trophy hundreds of yards away. He can guess at your odds of finding something better in the remaining days of the hunt.

But then he is silent, finished, as Joe Blackburn was right now. It was my move. I studied the magnificent animal across the canyon—solid, majestic, jaws chewing slowly, head drooping now and then as he dozed in the midday sun. More than worthy for my first bighorn sheep, on my first sheep hunt.

I eased my head away from the binoculars and turned it toward Joe, who was already watching me, and nodded. He nodded back, and grinned in agreement that my decision was the one he would have made. Anticipating that would be the case, he had made a mental programming of our next move, and by word and gesture indicated that I should follow him, move slowly, and stay low.

The move was a short one. The top of the ridge where we lay was itself a fine shooting position, except that a rifleman up enough to shoot would be silhouetted against the skyline. It was to eliminate the probability of spooking the ram that we slid over the crest plus twenty yards more on the downslope. Those few feet also took us from the bare ridgecrest into a fringe of trees, whose shadows would help mask any movement.

"Take your time. He hasn't moved."

Heeding the admonition, I wriggled around seeking a comfortable, steady prone position, and finally the ram came into view under the crosshairs. But shaky, even with the sling in place. Nervous? Perhaps just a bit. Excited? Damn right! But a more basic cause was at the root of my trembling: tension.

Lying on the downslope, head below my feet, it was impossible to bring the rifle to bear on the sheep except by assuming an awkward, strained position. Maybe you can get the shot off in good fashion, Gresham, and maybe you can't. Take a minute. Find a better spot.

A few yards to my right was a tree whose roots formed a fairly level structure on the hillside, and although the move required crossing a bare area bathed in sunlight, I whispered to Joe my intention to make it. I was halfway there when his hissing *"Hold it!"* froze me in mid-crawl. *"He's looking right at you! For gawd's sake, don't move."*

It must have been a routine surveillance on the part of the

ram, rather than an awareness that I was there, since he soon turned his head and resumed his siesta. At Joe's command I completed the move and snuggled into the position, which was superb. Now the crosshairs were rock-steady, with roots, tree trunk and sling affording an almost bench-rest situation. One final question. How far?

Three-fifty. The figure snapped into mind, to be parlayed with the knowledge that the 150-grain bullet from the 7mm Remington Magnum was on the money at 300 yards. "I think I'll hold on his backline." I whispered the comment-query across to Joe, who already knew how my rifle was sighted in.

"No!" his answer came quickly back, obviously from a man who had already considered the range and disagreed. "I believe I'd hold right on. Looks like about three hundred."

So the die was cast; the time had come! No more problems to be solved, mountains to climb, decisions to make. I thought the distance was greater, but I would, of course, accept Joe's judgment. Now there was no delay.

The polished bolt pushed a live cartridge from magazine into the chamber, then clicked into locked position with that soft, solid metallic sound. A deep breath, a normal one, let some out and hold it, touch it off! Maybe ten seconds for the whole operation, the "wrap" of a year or more of planning, plotting and working. As the light, velvet-smooth trigger, which I had come to know and love so well over many years, reached the release point, crosshairs hanging just behind the ram's shoulder, midway between his backline and his belly line, the bighorn turned his head full face in my direction.

The shot was off, exactly on schedule. Perfect release. Yet I watched in disbelief as the sheep rose to his feet and took a few steps to disappear over the ridge. He had vanished, even before the rolling echoes of the magnum ceased to bounce from canyon walls.

High on a Windy Hill! Except for the sighing of the wind through the spruce trees overhead, the silence of the high mountains was complete. Through the scope there was nothing but bare hillside. Binoculars. Still nothing. No ram slumped dead in his bed. No ram tumbling down into the canyon. No ram!

Maybe there never was. Are you still back in the heart of Louisiana, about to wake from a dream . . . a recurring dream that had often placed you high on a western mountain, squeezing one off on a bighorn ram? The pungent fragrance of burned gunpowder drifting up from the action of my rifle said no. No dream. Outfitter Joe Blackburn, five yards away, finally, reluctantly, made it official.

"You must've missed him!"

Again, complete silence. No more words were there. A comment such as that, from a veteran like Joe who was watching through binoculars, had an overwhelming chance of being 100 percent true. I accepted it, baffled, speechless, continuing aimlessly to search the panorama which lay out front.

"He didn't seem to be hit," Joe tried again, minutes later. "If the bullet had been low I think I'd have seen dust fly. If you were quite high that would explain it, since the bullet would have passed over the ridge." Joe shook his head as if he couldn't buy this latter theory, although it was the only one that made sense.

"I'll go over and take a look," he went on. "You stay here and stay ready. If the ram comes out over that second ridge you'll get another shot—that's about five-hundred yards or a bit more. Even out to that third ridge you might have a go at him, but that's a good eight-hundred. Make sure he doesn't slip over the ridge without you seeing him. It'll take me awhile."

With that he was gone, side-hilling his way down the steep canyon side. I watched him only for seconds, then swung the binoculars up to cover the distant ridges.

"You blew it! Two thousand miles by plane, twenty-five by horseback, too many on foot . . . and now this! Beautiful!"

The exhilaration was gone. The strength and vigor of adrenalin-charged veins had given way to fatigue. Quite suddenly I was bone-weary, with some reason.

On the day before we had ridden horseback for miles down a ridge which led from our high, dry sheep camp. Here and there we caught a glimpse of the twisting, shimmering line far below which was the Middle Fork of the Salmon River. Then we had walked, and sat, and glassed, and walked, and glassed. And had spotted four rams.

They were far, far away, but because we had seen them just as they were bedding down, Joe elected to give it a try. Four hours later—four hours of climbing, clawing and sliding—we reached the saddle which would look down on the sheep. That was one of the cupboards which we found bare, but the real crusher was in how very close we had been to success. Joe's assistant, watching through a spotting scope from far away, said we had missed the sheep by five minutes. They had not spooked, but had simply finished their siestas and moseyed away.

"The Middle Fork country," Jack O'Connor once told me, "is the roughest sheep country on the North American continent."

After that unsuccessful four-hour stalk it took us five hours to climb back to our horses, and another hour to ride to camp. It was time enough, for me, to reflect on and agree with Jack's opinion of that rugged, beautiful, awesome region.

A movement on the opposite slope caught my eye. It had taken Joe half an hour to reach the spot where the ram had been, and through the glasses I watched him pause to examine the bed. Hat in hand, he scrutinized every foot of the area, intuitively aware that I was with him via spirit and binoculars.

Nothing! No blood; no hair! It was pointedly evident in the dejected slope of Joe's shoulders as he followed the tracks of the ram those few feet from the bed to the crest of the ridge. Ever cautious, he peered over.

INSTANT JOY! Straightening and whirling toward me at the same time, Joe Blackburn swept his hat out, up and over in an unmistakable gesture which said, "Come on over! Here he is!"

A proud Rocky Mountain bighorn ram, lung-shot and with one shoulder broken, had walked those few feet across the ridge crest and out of sight before dropping dead. Far enough to give a novice sheep hunter a slight case of heart attack.

In the years since then that ram has looked down at me from my office wall, with a constant twinkle in his glass eyes which says, "Fooled you, didn't I?"

Horns of Gold, Hair of Snow

JOHN JOBSON

Our laden Beaver bush plane came in fast, under power, landing loonlike on a shimmering, tiny lake. The Yukon mountains towering above quite likely held at that time the richest Dall sheep pastures in North America. Happily free of his outsize load, the pilot taxied to the far end of the sparkling tarn, turned, and leaned on the throttle, causing the airframe to quiver and the powerful radial engine to roar. Almost at once the pontoons bit the water, the faithful ship lifted breathtakingly free at beachline, its floats brushing a stand of far-north spruce. The wings triumphantly waggled and we breathed again.

"Well," sighed the Old Outfitter, biting his lower lip, "we're here." And so we were, for forty-five days. Talking that pilot (a sport, and my fast friend since) into risking his aircraft in my behalf was the final (I hoped) organizational hurdle in an incredible accumulation of frustrations afflicting me at one point with colitis, an onset of shingles, and incipient pulsating cheek-twitch. A sucker for nostalgia, I had foolishly approached a partially "business" transaction from the romantic view, and it had taken some overdue luck to salvage the operation.

Since boyhood, I'd yearned to collect a trophy Dall ram. That king with golden, full-circle, flared-tipped crown and glittering ermined coat. A huge, blocky, thick-necked roman-nose specimen. A forty-three- or forty-four-incher, I told myself. Not to best the other guy, at all. Because for decades I'd loved the animal, and I wanted one of my own, to have and to cherish through the years. Seeing his noble head on my den wall would make my existence fuller. Rich and fulfilled.

A forty-three-inch Dall ram has never been anything like certain to deliberately plan, go for, and acquire. It was a lot easier then than now, but with old wise rams, lots can go wrong. Logistics should be coldly calculating. A combination of expert counsel, experience, ability, and benign fortune thrown in, like Patton going after Rommel, say. You cannot guarantee yourself that initial planning and subsequent tactical execution will put you and that one ram at the same place at the same time. The learned man gives it his best (excusing the term) shot, and collects talismans, amulets and scarabs. Men who love the grand, wild beasts and the thrill of seeking them know what I'm talking about.

Not unacquainted with North American sheep, I'd bagged several desert rams (which due to singular circumstances had come to me early), two bighorn, and one fair Stone. The game was sort of turning out, you might say, that I was working north to the one I wanted most. I'd been north—had even seen Dalls (and Fannin) from the highway. I could have harvested an average white ram, but didn't. It came one day that things seemed to jell, as they do if you're lucky. And I went after my Dall monarch with my heart, not my head.

Not only did I want to hunt the most likely sheep pastures

available then, I wanted the all-time classic white-ram guide. Back in the late 1920s and early 1930s my father had raved about one colorful, spectacularly successful guide, famous in articles and books. Dad's regard and enthusiasm for him was permanently contagious. I never forgot the name, or that Dad had said if he hunted Dall sheep, his ideal, perfect arrangement would be to have this man as his guide.

My little sister Jeanne, who lived in Washington, D.C., got me Xerox copies of old outdoor-magazine articles on this fellow from about World War I up till 1928. I went at them like a lady bug after an aphid, and my enthusiasm fanned anew, to Bessemer-furnace temperature. The Old Outfitter was still alive. He would be the lacy frosting on the dream-hunt cake. His letters were lucid, logical, and brimming with promise. The fact that he had no recent references I chose to ignore, feeling that belaboring this gauche detail was akin to asking Bette Davis to make a screen test for a TV cameo appearance.

Expert Yukon hunter-sportsmen insisted he'd been over the hill since V-8s replaced the Model A. My wife worried. "Why don't you get someone more up-to-date? Younger? *Recommended?*"

I explained it would mean ever so much to me to get my big ram with him. "He's old," I soothed, "but big rams are best found with a wise head, not fast feet."

Along the Alaska Highway, we heard disturbing rumors that the Old Outfitter was a has-been. Too many hills, too much grog, the frost of too many winters on his shoulders, we heard. On the scene, with mounting apprehension, we went into the game department to pay respects and purchase a license (alien). The Director of Fish and Game, a kind gentleman named Jeff Bidlake, asked me who my outfitter was. I told him. He threw up his hands.

"Oh my, Mr. Jobson," he shook his head. "He has no outfitter's license. We haven't renewed it. He has horses left, all right, and some gear, but with his drinking problem . . . he disappears, you see. He has kept clients cooling their heels for two weeks, here in town, while he recovers from a bender. Has no credit, no supplies. He's in some minor difficulty with the police. He's insulting to clients. And we have had it up to here with complaints."

My wife and I looked at each other. No Elmer Sizzle supersalesman I, and it's questionable if that would have worked with Mr. Bidlake anyway. But he kindly listened to my earnest plea; and he took my ambitions, inherited from Dad, seriously. We called my friend and boss Ted Kesting in New York City, and Ted told him I was a pillar of honest young manhood and that he would guarantee responsibility for any untoward cost to the Yukon government that this impending fiasco might bring about. I talked with the police and a couple of merchants. Mr. Bidlake told me to send the Old Outfitter in to him, with *money*. They had a terse, crystal-clear, mostly one-sided conversation while I tactfully strode the hall like an expectant father. The Old Outfitter had license and supplies.

My next chore was to buddy up to the highly independent bush pilot, who would no longer fly the outfitter *or* his clients. "You'll regret it," he told me.

These few preparations took longer than it takes to tell— several days, in truth. But sober and with a bit of scratch, the Old Outfitter was a goin' outfit—a backwoods organizational genius, a T. R. Roosevelt of decisive action. He had dispatched two guides, two wranglers, and upward of thirty-five horses to our rendezvous, where the bush plane landed on the beautiful little lake. Tents were up, caches were built, dining table had been constructed from aromatic spruce. Kitchen shelves groaned with ample supplies, and sweet-scented blue woodsmoke spiraled lazily from the three camp stovepipes. Our homey sleeping tent had been pitched right over fresh grizzly tracks.

The Old Outfitter was in his element. A side glance and the hired help jumped. That camp was run like an admiral's flagship. I could see straightaway that this man was on top of his job, and I also could understand why, when pinned down in town, civilization, he might drink to excess and be crotchety. "This is our main base camp," he told us. "Out of here we'll hunt grizzly and moose. But first"—his eyes twinkled—"you want to see if the old has-been can get you up to a forty-five-inch ram, eh?" He expertly rolled a cigarette. His touch was sure. "Tomorrow we'll take horses and climb these mountains into sheep country. Prob'ly camp up there ten days or more."

The young guide who led the pack train on the ascent the next morning had quite a sense of humor. His saddle horse slipped on some treacherously loose rock and they both came hurtling past us, a juggernaut of flailing hooves, ricocheting stones and divots. He stood, gave his clothing a token brushing, cupped his hands and yelled, "Don't go *that* way!"

On top we soon came to a lovely broad valley, and for miles we followed its greenhouse-lush floor. Regal Osborn caribou bulls, atop crests, were finely etched against opalescent pastel skies. A familiar place for them, in the insect-discouraging wind. At least seven lone monstrous *Alces gigas* bull moose, here and there, were feeding in the three-foot-tall yellowish dwarf willow and red ground-cover birch which mottled the mountainsides in delicate patterns. The moose's immensely long legs made them stand out as plain and tall as if they'd been on a clipped lawn. They looked *black,* and their huge antlers were being scraped of velvet, leaving alternate bloody and pure-white patches. The light colors would be bark-stained brown before long. Two mama grizzlies with cubs and one ponderous boar, unknown to each other, were busily plucking the hillside's fecund, mammary-like curves for succulent roots and juicy rodents. It was Shangri-la.

My wife turned and spoke. "Have you ever seen such an amount of game?" The Old Outfitter, ahead of Ann, turned with a speculative look. He did not approve of talk on the trail, even though this game to him was merely incidental. He was a *ram* guide.

We made a wilderness camp at the head of a draw right at the timberline, so that we'd have firewood for the sheepherder stoves used for cooking and heating. There were several comfortable tents, half the size of those at the main camp thousands of feet below. We had a willing, hardworking crew. It was a happy camp, a camp with the smell of success.

Out of here the Old Outfitter took me on horseback into proven sheep pastures, undulating sweeps of seemingly limitless country beneath somber skies, reminding me of the moors in *Wuthering Heights.* Instead of heather, it was covered with a curly short grass much like buffalo grass of the Montana high plains. We'd ride out for two, three, and four hours and glass for rams. We saw a multitude of sheep, and one day in a snow squall, the O.O. pointed out forty-odd ewes, lambs, and young rams grazing near some boulders.

"For practice," he smirked, "I'll stalk you into the center of that bunch of sheep. Follow me and do as I say."

A little over a half-hour, by gum, there we were, too, with

puzzled sheep all around us. This was, if not a truly hard life, at least tedious. Riding out for up to four hours, hunting for seven or eight hours with another interminable ride in darkness, was making us hollow-eyed from lack of sleep and giving us irritable nerves and testy digestion. We saw mature rams in pairs and threes, and singles, that hovered around forty inches.

"You won't settle for anything less than forty-four inches, eh," the Old Outfitter mused in an approving tone. He didn't wait for me to answer. "Tomorrow you and me'll take a really light mountain outfit and go to a spot I know. I had a German count there in 1920, but I don't take hardly anyone there, ever."

Leading a pair of packhorses, we rode up and out for what was our longest day so far. We had an old two-man "silk" tent, spartan supplies, little bundles of cut firewood, and a diminutive stove made with a jackknife from a five-gallon oil tin. Our Hillary-type camp was alpine, more moss and lichens than grass. We saw no rams at all. Even sign was a year old. Fogs came upon us that billowed in like the London ones of Sherlock Holmes' obscuring the East India Docks.

Twice we lost our camp, and never-ceasing hours of howling winds swept vicious particles of icelike snow against us. Our faces were bombarded until they were hamburgered raw, and I felt like screaming for it to stop. Supplies dwindled to chocolate candy, tea, and tobacco.

One day we were standing with our backs to the wind, the loyal saddle horses hunched miserably. "This," said the O.O., "is no time to be huntin' sheep. If we had any brains, especially you, Jobson, we'd hotfoot it back to timberline camp." I asked him to give it one more day. He beat his gloved hands together and shook his head mournfully.

Next afternoon the winds died and we crossed a great basin and came to a hitherto concealed ravine. Too steep to ride, we slipped and slid to a roaring alpine creek, waded it, got a grip on ourselves, and heroically clambered up the opposite "wall."

At the top, the Old Outfitter peeked over and almost had a stroke. He motioned me to his side. "Take off your hat and take a look," he whispered, highly agitated.

It is facetiously said that the only way to tell the size of trophy horns or antlers is to shoot the beast and put a steel tape

on him. This may be true if the trophies are on the edge of being good, flirting with the lowest third in the record book. It's never true with rare, exceptionally huge trophies. An outstanding one bellows like a bullhorn that it's one in thousands. There is no mistaking it.

I was looking into an Old Man's convention, the ram equivalent of London's Boodle Club on St. James's. Seven magnificent monsters—immense, blocky as bighorns, with huge-based horns circling and then flaring out, out . . . way out with unbroomed tips. They looked like *Ovis poli*. Each, a trophy hunter's Grail.

Our binoculars on them confirmed our estimate. "The biggest, third from left, will go an easy forty-seven," the Old Outfitter murmured. "Maybe forty-eight. All are record-book, but go for him. There's not one there less than forty-three or forty-four."

Drenched in perspiration, I was trembling, breathing heavily—gasping, really—from a combination of things. The arduous climb, the lack of decent nutrition, and the near hunt-climax sight of those awesome rams was enough in itself to prostrate me. Like others of certain strain of English descent, in emergency I'm inclined at least to act cool, nervousness coming after the event. But now I wondered. "Get a grip on yourself," I thought. "Remember Dad is watching you. You've hit woodchucks much farther off than those rams. Be calm. It'll soon be over." I checked the rifle to see if a cartridge was in the chamber. I wiped the lenses of the scope. I took the tape off the muzzle.

"That's right," the outfitter counseled, in perfect control. "Rest. Lay on your back til you get your wind."

My hands still trembled with fatigue. At that split-second the fan was hit. Another giant ram, a lookout, strolled unconcernedly from behind a little rise, above, on his way to join the others, possibly for his relief, when he casually glanced in our direction, did a Pangborn double-take, came down with his legs making a Disney buzz-saw blur. Intuitively the other seven were galloping all-out. The biggest ram was covered by two others, but a good one indeed, probably forty-five inches, was coming up behind, and the Old Outfitter, nearly out of his mind, wildly raged, "Second from last! Second from last! Now last! *Shoot shoot shoot . . . !*"

I had some low-growth in front of the scope, so I leaped to my feet. An offhand proposition. Then, I could not for the life of me find that damned reticule. It was a split spider-web with an infinitesimal tiny black dot. Great for California ground squirrels, but not for Yukon rams going like Arab steeds. The third shot, that forty-five-inch ram rolled like a Western movie horse on the end of a flying-W snare.

"HOORAY!" cried the Old Outfitter.

At this point my .270 with Mauser action jammed. The ram got groggily to his feet, ran toward us, saw his mistake, turned and took off after the others, who by now, being so unbelievably old and fat, were laboring along in dreadful difficulty. But they kept going, and in spite of some staggering, and their alarmingly heaving sides, they made good time.

"Hell!" the Old Outfitter bitterly stormed. "You hit that one's *horns!* Of all the . . .." A sob escaped him!

I ran over the crest a bit, sat, got a good steady position, and fired my last two rounds. Each a heartbreaking miss. Spare ammunition was on the horses, by now 400 yards behind. The noise had spooked them. The rams disappeared at last. Out of range anyway, the bunch had waited for the straggler. Together they dipped over a crest, a thousand yards from us. My brief moment of truth had come and gone, and I'd failed. The rams had won. I doubt if a matador in Madrid's bull ring who had missed his thrust and, worse, gotten gored in full view of thousands of *aficionados* would have felt worse.

And the Old Outfitter. He'd done his part, as Dad said he would, and more, after all. He was still, silent, gazing blankly, like in shock.

I cleared my throat. "Well," I attempted, "another day, eh."

"Those rams are *gone,*" he growled. "Country too rough to ride to."

"Well, maybe next year then."

He shook his head, punishing himself, and me. "This is their last season. Too old. A bad winter's coming. They'll never make it. Many wolves around. I never in my life seen that many record rams together at once. That was once-in-a-lifetime."

"Well," I said, "I guess we better go."

The Old Outfitter, incidentally, went on to a decade of successful outfitting before he retired with honors. At that, it might be best for upcoming sheep hunters to choose a young, gung-ho outfitter brimming with recent references. Or would it?

Beyond the Himalayas

ELGIN GATES

Individual snowflakes come slanting out of the dark sky as we reach the two stone shepherd's huts at the foot of Wad Khun pass. With me are eighteen men of Hunza—Hunzakuts, they are called—and three half-tamed yaks. This is the third day of forced marching. During the last sixteen hours since leaving the main trail we have covered nineteen miles of difficult terrain. The dim tortuous trail has led across perilous sixty-degree slopes, through labyrinths of shattered moraine and creaking glacial ice. According to my altimeter, the altitude has varied between 10,000 and 12,500 feet.

I am deep in the heart of Central Asia in a lofty region known as *Bam-i-dunya,* the legendary roof-of-the-world. It is a land of spectacular beauty; of misty, hidden valleys and magnificent snowy mountains in the kingdom of Hunza, a tiny state between Afghanistan and West Pakistan on the Red Chinese border.

It is a land of danger, of massive, grinding glaciers and thundering avalanches; of shrieking winds and merciless storms; uninhabited by mankind.

It is the abode of that mythical creature the abominable snowman; it is the home of the giant wild sheep, *Ovis poli,* the most magnificent big-game trophy on the face of the earth—the Holy Grail of every hunter in the world and the prize that has brought me to this remote country beyond the Himalayas.

Within minutes after our arrival at Wad Khun, a strong wind comes whistling down from the pass, bringing a torrent of dry snow pellets with it. Fifteen of the men take refuge in the larger hut. Four of us crawl into the other hut. With me is Sultan Ali, my interpreter, and Sheree Ali Khan and Aman Shah, the two Hunza shikaris. Aman Shah is the only man in the party who has been in this rugged country before. Long ago, he once journeyed to the Chinese border.

I unroll my sleeping bag and crawl into it, clothes and all, as the men kindle a tiny fire against the opposite wall and brew tea. I wonder if Herb Klein, my hunting companion, has been caught in the storm. He is hunting in another valley far to the south at a lower elevation.

As I drink the second cup of hot tea, the storm breaks upon us—a monstrous, raging storm. The wind rises to a screaming crescendo and beats against the hut with cyclonic fury. The fire is snuffed out and cannot be rekindled. I manage to light a stub of candle inside a small bottle. By its dim flickering light I watch in fascination and dread as snow pellets come spilling through the rock walls to form pyramids on the floor.

Is this the end of the line? Would we have a prayer of fighting our way back to the main trail through nineteen miles of deep snow?

The only entrance into this mysterious land is through a narrow, green-terraced valley in the tiny kingdom of Hunza, sometimes called Shangri-la. Precise details of the country beyond Hunza are unknown. Maps are marked with the cryptic note: *Not fully explored.*

We had planned to be in Hunza in September for this hunt, but because of political problems in Karachi where our permits were issued, the expedition had been delayed a full month. It was late October when we finally reached Gilgit, the northernmost outpost of the old British colonial empire in Kashmir, now part of Pakistan.

In four days we marched sixty-five miles from Gilgit through the Hunza valley to Baltit, where we were cordially welcomed by Mir Mohammed Jamal Khan, the ruler of Hunza. When I told him of my desire to journey into the high country beyond the Himalayas to hunt for *Ovis poli,* he warned me of the dangers that lay ahead.

"Winter is coming and there will be terrible storms and avalanches. If you get trapped in deep snow, you cannot escape. There is no food except what little you can carry with you and the game you can bag."

Sleep would not come that night, and I lay awake for hours in sober thought of the ordeal ahead.

It is now October 29, far too late to be marching into an unknown region. Speed is essential if I am to have any chance of success. I must get to the high country and back as quickly as possible.

October 30   The early sun slants in from a deep blue sky, warm and brilliant, as I make the final adjustments on my saddle. The Mir comes over and puts his arm around my shoulder. "I will be praying for your success. Beware of Chinese patrols. They sometimes cross over the passes and come several miles down into Hunza territory."

I acknowledge his concern and thank him for the help he has given me. We part with a handshake. I say goodbye to Herb Klein, not knowing just when or if I will ever see him again.

With Sultan Ali leading, we head up the trail at a swift canter. The Mir has provided us with the best horses available. We soon pass Ghulkin glacier. It comes down from Batura peak, which towers 25,450 feet. I look up at the massive icebound summit and shudder as I remember what the Mir told me yesterday. *This is the peak where the five German climbers were killed. They were the only other outsiders to enter the Hunza valley this year.*

Abruptly the sun is blotted out. I look up to see a solid charcoal sky. A strong wind strikes us head on, and within a mile snowflakes come sweeping in. We canter the horses when the trail allows and dismount and lead them up the steep, rugged traverses.

There is four inches of snow on the ground when we reach Khaibar. The valiant horses are finished. I unroll my sleeping bag in the rest house and fall asleep, exhausted. Altitude 8800 feet, temperature 18° F., distance 22 miles.

October 31

I learn that Sultan Ali has been given unlimited authority by the Mir to commandeer anything we need. He also has instructions to hand-pick sixteen of the best men in the valley. Fresh horses are being saddled outside as I drink hot tea.

Seven of us ride out of Khaibar. The new men ride with straight-backed pride. They are splendid fellows with flashing eyes and unconcealed elation at being among the chosen few. It is almost dark when we reach Sost, the last Hunza village in the valley. There is great excitement at our arrival. Altitude 9100 feet, temperature 26°, distance 21 miles.

November 1

A big crowd is gathered around the rest house. Sultan Ali tells me the last eight men have been chosen. We also have three yaks which will carry most of our food supply, but all of us will be walking. The rest of our supplies are divided into small packs of about twenty-five pounds each for the Hunzakuts.

Even though we are walking now, our pace is swift. We are climbing through steep defiles and across rock slides. The yaks are marvelous animals. They go through difficult terrain a horse would never attempt. Around us, snowy peaks dominate the horizon, and the near landscape is a chaos of boulder-strewn slopes. It is nearly dark when we reach the shepherd's huts at Wad Khun. Altitude 11,000 feet, temperature 32°.

November 2   Last night was the ordeal of the great storm. This morning the wind has abated. Fortunately, most of the dry snow has been scoured away by the screaming north wind, leaving the ground bare and dark.

Following the dim trail, climbing slowly, with extreme caution, we reach the top of the frigid pass and have to chop our way through the narrow ice-blocked defile. I check the altimeter as we pause to rest. 14,400 feet.

We start the descent, traversing back and forth on the perilous slope. Crossing a steep shale slope, Aman Shah shouts a warning. We run for our lives, reaching a buttress of solid rock just as a churning river of snow and shale comes pouring by. None of the men is caught, but one of our yaks is swept down the precipitous chasm and buried forever. It is late afternoon when we find shelter under the overhanging ledge of a gigantic boulder. Food will be rigidly rationed. We huddle together under the ledge, keeping tiny willow-and-*burtsa* fires burning. *God help us if there is a heavy snowfall!* Altitude 13,100 feet, temperature 8°, distance about 15 miles.

November 3   We are still camped under the ledge. Today I hunted ibex in a side valley to supplement our food supply and was successful in bagging two. Time is very critical now. I wonder how much longer this capricious high-altitude weather will hold off.

November 4   We push eastward up a narrow gorge and pause to watch a cascade of sun-silvered water surging down a precipitous slope rising thousands of feet to a blue-white glacier. I am enthralled by the sheer grandeur of this vast and inaccessible region of the roof-of-the-world. There always has been a burning desire inside me to climb the high mountains. Long ago, I reached an altitude of 19,050 feet in the Rupshu range, 300 miles southeast of here. *Once, just once before I die, I want to climb to 20,000 feet.* But even this is second to the all-consuming desire to reach my own Mecca, the home of *Ovis poli*.

At four o'clock we reach the last stone hut at Kuksell, six miles from Khunjerab and Chapchingal passes—and the Chinese border. At seven o'clock the temperature is –9°. Altitude 15,450 feet.

November 5

It is four-thirty a.m. and still dark. Temperature –14° as we wait for the dawn. I will take Sultan Ali, the two shikaris, and one of the yaks.

We struggle up a steep incline for perhaps two miles and come to a bend in the canyon. Rounding it, I can see that the valley broadens out into rolling hills and open meadows that lead to the distant passes. We reach the shelter of a low, rocky ridge and stop to rest. I train my binoculars toward the passes. There they are—Khunjerab to the right, Chapchingal to the left. I search the slopes leading to Khunjerab for about ten minutes, then turn my binoculars toward the higher pass of Chapchingal.

Suddenly, I freeze. Silhouetted against the dark sky on a distant crest stands a magnificent *Ovis poli* ram! His great flaring horns make a full curl, then turn down at the tips. My hands tremble and I have to lower the binoculars. I am not ashamed to say that tears of emotion run down my face. Here is a sight that few living men have been privileged to see, the fabulous *Ovis poli* in its natural habitat. Here, finally, is my rendezvous with destiny. At this moment I am fully repaid for every step of the ninety-five miles of forced marches through the stupendous mountain ranges that barred the way; all the hunger and hardships of the trail; the cruel relentless toil over the terrible glacial moraines and around the sinister crevasses; the exhausting struggle through the driving snows and the bitter, howling winds of the icebound passes that had to be crossed.

Controlling my emotion with an effort, I raise the binoculars again and feast my eyes on the distant ram. His remarkable horns will measure well over sixty inches. Other rams come over the ridge. There is a whole herd of them! Quickly, I appraise the possibilities of making a stalk.

Nearby, there is a shallow, ice-gouged swale. I leave Sheree Ali Khan there with the yak. Then I lead Aman Shah and Sultan Ali behind a vertical ridge where we will be hidden from the *poli,* and we start the climb.

For three hours, we struggle slowly upward into the permanent snowfield, threading our way around jagged pinnacles of rock. Far below, the rams have bedded down.

Breathing is difficult; climbing becomes an agonizing ordeal. We stop to rest often, gasping for air. We climb a few yards at a time, breathing deeply three or four times with each step, fighting to get enough oxygen into our starving lungs. Summoning our last reserves of strength and willpower, we move upward, step after desperate step toward a snowy saddle.

Finally, there is nothing above. We collapse on the hard snow at the top of the saddle. There is a gentle slope leading down the other side. We can descend all the way and be in a perfect position for a stalk on the rams. The temperature is −18°. I pull out my altimeter and stare at it in disbelief. It reads 20,800 feet. It is a fine Swiss high-altitude instrument calibrated to 22,000 feet. I shake it and look again. The reading is the same, 20,800 feet! *Unwittingly, I have attained one of my long-cherished goals—to climb to 20,000 feet once before I die!*

This unnamed saddle is higher than any point on the North American continent! No wonder the final stages of our climb were so agonizing.

Hours later, we reach a vantage point behind a ridge where I hope the rams are still bedded down. But no! Aman Shah touches my shoulder and points. There are the rams, about 500 yards away, trotting over a ridge into China. Somehow they must have sensed our presence in some unknown way. A terrible wave of despair sweeps through me. Then, as I watch them disappear, a final hope is born. The last seven or eight rams stop near the top of the slope and look back. I quickly decide to try a shot.

Moving around a boulder, I rest the rifle and my left hand on it, and take aim at what appears to be the ram carrying the longest horns. My rifle is sighted in for 300 yards. Ballistically, the bullet will be 22½ inches low at 500 yards. I allow for this and with a prayer gently squeeze the trigger.

The chosen ram takes two or three leaps up the slope, then collapses and rolls down to the bottom. At last I have an *Ovis poli* ram! I begin shouting with joy. The great quest is at an end! The men catch my enthusiasm and we embrace each other, then rush down the long slope where the ram lies in the snow.

Other than the long-ago museum expedition, this is the first *Ovis poli* to be taken by an American trophy hunter. I am jubilant as I fondle the great, curling horns. The ram is in splendid condition. His heavy body is light-brown on the back, shading to gray speckled with white. The heavy white winter ruff on his neck is fully four inches long.

For me, the dream of a lifetime has been fulfilled. The Mecca of any man is, in the greater sense, but the epitome of desire in his soul. Deep in the heart of Asia, on a lofty, wind-blown slope of the roof-of-the-world, I came at last to my own Mecca and found the rams of Shangri-la. The hunter's horn has called and I have gone.

One More Step

JOHN WOOTERS

It was a bad place in spite of its wild beauty, but the sun was already setting and we had no time to look for a better place for the business we had come to do. The four of us were standing in the head of a canyon, high up in an obscure mountain range along the border of the Mexican states of Tamaulipas and San Luis Potosí. To reach this place we had traveled first by light aircraft, then by truck, then by Jeep, then on horseback, and finally on foot as we had macheted our way up through the jungled canyon. No *norteamericanos* had ever come here before, and possibly no modern men of any breed. There was really no reason to come here to this fierce, wild, remote, lovely spot except to meet its fierce, wild, lovely king, the American jaguar.

We stood in a small, semi-level opening no more than twenty feet square, floored with an ankle-breaking cobbling of rocks and boulders. On three sides rose sheer cliffs overhung with vines and tropical foliage. On the fourth side, downhill, the V of the canyon fell away, widening and deepening as it descended.

We gazed around us in the dusk, all thinking the same thought: This is a very good place for a man to be killed if things do not go just right. The two Mexicans settled themselves with backs against the base of the cliff. Rufus Hayes and I readied our rifles and tried to find some sort of solid footing on the boulders. Natividad, the ancient man of the mountains, watched us with Aztec impassiveness, thoughtfully stroking the rawhide drumhead of his *pujandero*. Darkness was coming swiftly; he could barely see my nodded signal to commence the drama.

Now he placed his hand inside the gourd body of his instrument and grasped the braided horsehair cord fixed to the center of the drumhead. Bearing down hard with a horny thumb, Don Nati pulled hard, allowing the braid to slip between his fingers. The sound that came forth would make a man's hair stand on end in Central Park at high noon; in this wilderness, in the hour of the owl, it generated waves of gooseflesh. It was the truculent, grunting challenge-call of a male jaguar.

It's a sound which, once heard, is stored permanently in a hunter's memory tapes, a sullen, coughing roar which dies away in a series of grunts like a coarse-toothed saw cutting into a coffin. You can feel it deep inside your chest and it seems to rattle your very soul.

We listened, thrilling, as Nati's call rolled out across the thicketed slopes around us, echoing briefly and diminishing to a silence so profound that it was almost shocking. The jaguar's call had instantly and totally hushed the mountain. Every bird, every animal, even every tree and rock, it seemed, held poised and breathless, listening and waiting.

In our canyon the blackness was now so absolute that Rufus and I, not even an arm's length apart, couldn't see each other. We also held motionless, our night-blinded eyes closed and jaws slacked, staring into the darkness with our ears. With the mountain and all its life, we waited.

The world stood perfectly still for a thousand or two years. Then, far out to our left and above us, we heard something. A small boulder clanked and began sliding and rolling down the slope, gathering momentum and cracking into brush and trees until at last the canyon swallowed it up. Then, only silence. But only a big animal could have dislodged that boulder, and we needed nothing more to know that the jaguar was there, that he had heard the challenge, and that he was coming.

It's important that you understand about jaguars: they are not real, flesh-and-blood animals at all, but only glowing phantoms living in the imagination of obsessed hunters. Hunting a jaguar soon ceases to be sport and becomes an act of dedication. I have hunted for nights and days and nights until, in my weariness, I could no longer separate night from day. Eating where I pause, sleeping only when overpowered by sleep, never really knowing where I am, or caring, I have hunted a jaguar until time blurred into numbness. On the first day of a jaguar hunt I am impatient to be after the beast, and full of anticipations. At the end of two days, the search has become a sort of compulsion. After three days and nights it is a grim religion, a pilgrimage, a crusade sans banners. On the fifth day comes the onset of a primitive fury. In six days my world has narrowed to only the jungle and the cat. Home, family, my entire way of life on the other side of the mountains has faded into fantasy; the jaguar—that fantastic cat I've never even glimpsed—has become the sole reality.

Within eight days I am reverted totally. That a jaguar may actually be slain is no longer even conceivable. Hope, expectation, and even desire have been replaced as a first principle by simple relentlessness. I am become Ahab. With the passage of yet more days, relentlessness can be elevated to an undeniable madness. And, after a fortnight, I can walk out of the jungle, haggard, bearded, empty-handed, and serene, as though purified by the sheer intensity of the quest.

In simplest terms, I have become quite possessed by these recluse cats who live always beyond the end of the road and whose unseen presence dominates a landscape like a thundercloud.

And now, on the ninth day of this hunt, Rufus and I stood

entombed in blackness and listened to the utter nothingness of sound as a jaguar stalked us.

For nine days we had camped in the valley of a lake locally named La Loca, the crazy one. During the rains this lake may grow to a length of almost ten kilometers, but when the rains cease, its bed of porous volcanic rock cannot contain the water and it drains away so that the lake recedes an average of eight or nine inches each day from its margins. A strange place to camp, beside a lake that runs away from you, but the signs of jaguar were all around us. Near our palm-thatched lean-to lay the remains of a horse colt killed and eaten a few days before we arrived. At night we could hear the brutes grumbling and coughing high up in the canyons above the lake, and most mornings, we could locate their awesome pug marks where the cats had come down to drink not far from camp. Once, while scouting single-file up a rocky draw at midmorning, we startled a jaguar out of his bed, so close that we plainly heard his soft-footed bounds as he ran up the trail just out of our sight. We even found his scratching trees, oozing sap from fresh gashes higher than our heads.

But we could not manage actually to see a jaguar despite dogged days and nights of searching.

We did find psychedelic red-and-silver squirrels, and trogons, cousins to the Aztecs' sacred quetzal bird. We did capture a boa, eight feet of gentle muscle sheathed in an opalescent coat of mail. We found whitetail deer in the thickets and teal on the lake and doves in the trees, all of which we killed when we needed meat. We watched troops of coatimundis foraging like monkeys in the palm crowns, and surprised jaguarundi cats on the trails at night, circling ember-eyed in our lights. Regularly we watched the mass flighting of wild parrots, flying always by twos and flashing green and yellow, rose and magenta and lilac in the westering sun. We saw that La Loca was a magical place, jaguar or no jaguar.

But we could *not* see a jaguar.

Until this ninth day, when we decided in desperation to brave the high canyons at twilight and try the *pujandero* (which is Spanish for "grunter"). Our rifles were equipped with powerful shooting lights, and the jungle around us made certain that any shot we might have would be a short one. If the cat came from above, anything less than a perfect killing shot would certainly dump a wounded 200-pound cat into the midst of four men on impossible footing. Yet if he came to us from below, he would surely get our scent; in the stillness we could already feel the evening-cooled air sliding down off the mountain, funneling into the V of the canyon. The big cats ordinarily pay little attention to the smell of a man, but four men at only a few paces might be too much even for the arrogance of a jaguar.

It was too late to worry about any of these things, however, for the challenge had been issued and accepted. We could only wait, fingering the switches of our lights and scanning the invisible jungle like bats. We knew the animal must be a male, for females do not respond to the *pujandero,* and we knew, having seen his tracks, that the male on this mountain was very big. Further, we knew for certain that the cat would be enraged at the sound of a rival male intruding in his territory and that he was coming to fight. What we did not know was when or from which direction he might choose to attack.

After ten minutes of bone-grating silence, Nati called again, briefly, and at once we heard the tinkling of pebbles as an animal moved swiftly across the slope about 100 yards to our left. By ear we were able to follow his route now as he turned sharply downhill to get into the canyon's notch below us. We strained to catch the almost inaudible sounds he made as he approached, and now we could hear them more and more plainly as he closed in. A rustle of palmetto against his flank, the grating of a rock underfoot, even a padded footfall. He was close, so close that if he came even one more step toward us it would be time for the light and the rifle.

But now the sounds ceased. The cat was poised, listening, scenting . . . then we heard, with heartbreaking distinctness, the expulsion of his breath as he spat, catlike, in disgust. He never took that one last step toward us; instead, the jaguar turned and went away and left us there in the crushing blackness of the Mexican night.

In an alpine meadow on another mountain, four years later and a thousand miles from La Loca, I met another beast, and it came to pass that his fate, too, finally hung upon the taking of one more step.

The mountain is part of the high, beautiful Sangre de

Cristo range a few miles from Taos, New Mexico. It was early October and the aspens still had their leaves. On the slopes across the valley they wound down the humps and shoulders of the mountain in yellow rivers, here and there forming pools or solitary splashes of saffron against the black-green timber. It's a fine time to be on a mountain with a trusted rifle slung to the shoulder. The elk are still rutting and bulls still bugle now and then. This is another of the unforgettable sounds of wilderness. It begins low and slides up the scale to end in a coarse, reedy squeal that conjures a picture of hard-knotted belly muscles, straining. No other sound I ever heard more vividly expresses all of nature's blind, resistless urgings. In a bull elk's bugle rings all the rage and lust and pride of sheer physical power that can be compressed into a thousand pounds of dumb masculine brute. Echoing from the mountain at dawn, it must stir whoever hears it to his roots.

It was a half-hour until dusk when the bull bugled in the meadow below where Jesse Williams and I were sitting. The sound snatched both of us up as though by our shirtfronts, and Jesse grabbed my knee and hissed, "There's a bull down there, and he's not a little one. You won't have much time to find him. He'll have cows around."

I nodded, shucking all my gear except rifle and binoculars. We hotfooted it down an abandoned logging road which slanted along the mountainside toward the sound of the bugle. Suddenly, Jesse pulled up short and pointed at two dark shapes far below us, in a golden meadow between the trees. "There're more off to the left," Jess said. "It's a big herd. I'll wait here; you'll have a better chance to get close by yourself."

As swiftly as I could move without making too much racket, I dropped into the timber and, fifteen minutes later, worked my way to the edge of the lower meadow. No more than five minutes of shooting light remained when I arrived at a stump across which I could rest the rifle to cover the clearing. It was full of elk . . . but a couple of quick scans of the herd showed that every animal in sight was a female. Desperately I swept the binoculars back and forth across the scene, seeking the cream-colored body and massive antlers of the herd bull, to no avail. I knew he was there, somewhere, but I simply could not see him. Helpless, I crouched there behind my stump and watched the last light fade swiftly into darkness. Then I rose and slipped away to meet Jesse. He told me that the bull had stood arrogantly in plain sight from his position above and that he had kept the binoculars on the animal in momentary expectation of seeing the bullet's impact. He reported that the bull was a big one, perhaps the one I'd traveled several thousand miles and spent three years trying to find.

We were back in the meadow at dawn, but the elk were gone. There was plenty of sign, but the animals had drifted up into the timber on the west ridge above us, into the tangled blowdown where no man alive can move quietly enough to take them by surprise. We triangulated the bull's position of the evening before and discovered that, from my stump, he had been concealed by three stunted spruces—the only spot in the whole meadow where I couldn't have seen him! The range had only been 150 yards.

After a thorough reconnaissance and council of war, we decided that this bull was worth hunting, that he hadn't been spooked, and that my best chance for a shot at him was to haunt this clearing at dawn and dusk, every day until I got him or until I had to leave for home. For two and a half more days I followed this plan, hunting the bull with diligence and discipline and devotion, but without luck. On the last afternoon of my time, the keen edge of anticipation was wearing away against fatigue and disappointment. Nevertheless, I went back to the meadow and settled myself into my now-familiar hideout among the roots of a blown-down spruce. Except for one mule deer doe and her fawn, it was a dull wait, and I caught myself almost drowsing as the shadows lengthened, just when I most needed my alertness.

Then, twenty minutes before ultimate dark, I heard a sound which wiped away the boredom in a split second: it was the unmistakable racket of a group of large animals trooping down toward my meadow from the ridge above, stirring leaves and snapping dry twigs like a platoon of cavalry. All at once I knew that this hunt was going to have a garrison finish; I *was* going to kill that mighty bull, and it was an exultation to think of it! I swung the rifle's muzzle to cover the upper end of the clearing and waited.

Then, after a few minutes of listening, all my joy went out

of me at once. The sounds of the elk were no longer approaching; instead, they were now diminishing. The herd had passed by my clearing, just out of sight in the dark timber, and were going uphill, toward the meadow in which Jesse and I had been that first evening when we heard the bull bugle. I was crushed, almost stunned, but I struggled to think out a tactic which still might retrieve the situation from disaster. I just might have time before dark to reach the upper meadow. It wasn't far, but was steeply uphill. I tried not to run, knowing that my sea-level lungs couldn't take a hard climb at 9,000 feet without having to rest—and there was no time to rest.

It was the longest climb I ever made. Despite my planning, I couldn't keep my feet from trotting as the sun went out of the sky. I prayed that I wouldn't run over some unseen deer and panic the whole mountainside, but it was too late for stealth and caution.

It was nearly dark as I slipped past the last trees on the lower edge of the meadow and saw four big animals out in the open. The binoculars told me they were cow elk.

"The son of a bitch has got to be here somewhere," I promised myself savagely. "He can't have that kind of luck twice. I *know* he's here . . . but where the hell is he?" With the rifle poised, thumb on the safety latch, I took one more long stride to bring more of the meadow into view.

The bull was there. He was standing at the edge of the timber hardly forty yards to my left, partly screened by a fallen log and all but invisible against the dark woods. As I made that one fateful stride, my attention still riveted on the cows, he exploded into flight. I whirled and dropped to one knee, frantically hoping for a snap shot in the seconds before he disappeared into the forest.

There was no chance at all. For one fragment of a second, as he galloped up the slope, I caught the silhouette against the pink-orange sky of great, branching antlers, more massive than I'd ever dreamed of. Then he vanished, and I could only kneel there and listen to the sounds of his retreat, crashing over the timbered ridges. Even in the midst of my anguish I was surprised that I could hear him running for so long, so far into the blowdown. But the noise died away, leaving the darkling meadow empty and lonely and suddenly cold around me. I knelt there a long time, and then rose wearily and started walking back downhill to my rendezvous with Jesse.

Now that it was over, somehow I felt at peace with this peaceful world about me, without any sense of defeat at all. As I walked I was thinking that to be present in a wilderness is to possess it for the time being, and a little of it for all time. In the same way, to be so intensely involved with a wild animal, as I have been with a jaguar, or a bull elk, is to possess a fragment of his wildness forever. And it really doesn't matter whether he, or I, take one too many or one too few steps, or even whether either of us lives or dies today, for the sun will rise tomorrow and the seasons and centuries will roll on, and the mountain will make another jaguar or another elk bull because it is not complete without him. And men like me will come again to make our quest, and succeed or fail, and then go, taking always that one more step. And the mountain shall always watch and listen, and never tremble at our footfalls.

A Time for Muleys

CHARLES F. WATERMAN

There is this special time between brilliant autumn and the for-
bidding mountain winter. There still are days of rapid thaws,
but the Rockies remain white down past timberline and each
foreboding snowstorm has a false finality about it as if winter
had really closed in.

Most of the potholes are frozen, but mallards slant con-
fidently into steaming spring creeks and loaf on ice edges of the
larger rivers. At night there are sounds of Canada geese probing

for mountain passes, and most of the snows and blues have already passed on their way south.

Since the earliest deer and elk seasons of September the hunters have sagely stated that the game was high, somehow ignoring the fact that high to low can be a matter of only a few minutes' travel for a deer in case of suddenly bad weather.

The big muley bucks have been hard to find. In late summer some of them could be seen as burly shadows among lesser deer on the alfalfa fields at dusk, and when the season opened a few of them were brought in with pride—but when the first rifle reports bounced through the rocky canyons they had disappeared, as big bucks tend to disappear every fall. They lost interest in alfalfa fields and left most of the valley foraging to does, fawns, and simple-minded forkhorns. The middle-sized bucks were found frequently, but the big ones very seldom. Their broad and slightly splayed tracks might be seen in high rimrock, but the beds there would be empty when hard-breathing hunters arrived. Humans give the mule deer little credit for genius, but trophy males are individuals above their fellows in wit. It is not entirely chance that has given them time to grow heavy antler beams and thick shoulders.

There were several seasons when I hunted mule deer a great deal, more than I could afford to, but there was the excuse that we ate hardly any meat but venison for much of the year. My wife, Debie, had a more practical approach than I, and when game biologists reported that more does should be killed she shot one on the first day of one season, only to be treated coolly by hunters afflicted with a big-buck complex. She said, with sense, that the food locker was empty and that a young doe is prime meat.

Although the licenses called for two deer I usually approached the magical time between fall and winter without a kill, insisting that I was waiting for trophies, but knowing secretly that I was simply fearful of ending the hunt for another year.

There was the immense satisfaction of lying on a high sage ridge and feeling across the opposite slope with my binoculars to make out bedded deer. When I found one, continued search would almost invariably reveal more sage-hued forms. One slope might take an hour's study, and it was almost a relief to learn there were no worthwhile bucks so that I could go on to another ridge.

One October there was the Montana giant who rested repeatedly in a brushy canyon notch that could be viewed from above, apparently a poor place for bedding, but he could escape like a slipping whitetail through small, thick conifers while I stared watery-eyed at the general area, a chilly canyon wind whipping at my exposed perch. Once I had seen the tines of his antlers moving among some alders along a creek lower down. It took several trips before I learned his favorite escape route and posted Debie there. She caught only one glimpse of a dark, silent form sliding through heavy cover. Several days later she and Jack Ward tried it together, and this time the big buck elected to go with a thumping rush along the canyon wall and Jack's quick .270 caught him center with a single bang while I was still gathering the rocks with which I planned to flush him out.

This other time, Debie, the provider, had collected a butter-fat, rag-horned muley for the locker. We had been looking for elk, and it was late evening with only minutes of shooting time remaining, and she had seen him with several does and fawns feeding in a poorly lighted draw. They sensed her presence and milled uncertainly while she took a steady shooting position, and then they started up a slope, where they alternately merged with juniper clumps and appeared plainly against drab autumn grass. Just below a crest the buck stopped for the muley's risky backward look and she fired once.

The fleeing herd noisily topped the ridge and disappeared, Debie's deer somewhere among them, and I arrived there in a few moments to find her small and forlorn in her bulky wool hunting pants and red shirt. It was almost dark and her deer was gone, she said, but it had looked like a good shot and how could she have missed? With the last light we found the fat buck just over the ridge, but the heavy bullet, chosen for elk, had not opened much on the way through and he had gone a bit farther than was to be expected. Debie was pleased but suddenly announced it was time she killed a trophy.

As the snowy time of the mule deer rut arrived that year I still clung to my two tags and we went to Montana's Madison range. In dead of winter the mule deer often feed fearlessly along the swift, shallow Madison in plain sight of the valley highways.

In late November they work up and down the slopes with weather changes. By then most of the hunting camps have been brought out of the highest mountains and outfitters plan to work from head-quarter ranches or from permanent camps at easy levels.

It is the up-and-down movement of deer that can make good hunting for observers of the game. When snow becomes too deep on the upper slopes the deer will move down to feed, but at first they do it mostly at night and return to high and difficult country during the day for alternate bedding and browsing. There are times when the foothill snow is webbed with trails but no daytime deer are present. As Bud Baker of Ennis explains it, the time for shooting is just after dawn when deer return to higher ground and a hunter who has slipped through them in darkness may cut them off with an ambush. The procedure is simple if the location and weather are right. We have tried it when it had turned too warm and much high snow had melted, and we found only areas packed with tracks where deer herds had been a day or two before. They had temporarily abandoned their valley visits.

In the November I remember so well, four of us left Baker's motel long before daylight. It was Bud and his wife, Mary Ann (for some forgotten reason called "Mike"), Debie, and I. Patches of crisp snow crunched under the four-wheel-drive's lugged tires as we got under way on an empty road, going up the valley in the cold starlight of early morning. One star shone so brightly near the blurred mountain tops that we argued whether it could be a man-made light but decided it was the wrong color for that.

We took a frozen side road and putted past Pete Durham's ranch house, dark and a little apart from the shadows of other buildings, and drew brief but noisy attention from the ranch dogs. We went through the barnyard and through a gate to the steep pasture slope, where the engine labored a little at the be-ginning of the mountain, and parked there to continue on foot.

On the snowy foothill shoulder were dark blobs of cattle that would wait until we were quite near and then startle us by jumping wildly in apparent terror, only to stop and stare after thirty feet of flight. Once we saw smaller, quicker shadows ahead and knew they were deer, good sign that many of the mu-leys were "down." After we found the irrigation-ditch crossing we walked carefully to avoid badger holes and were quiet as possible, for we knew we must be passing the deer's feeding areas. Suddenly the peaks ahead of us to the east showed in sharp outline from the very first morning light, and we began to make out the dark streaks of brush and tree-lined draws and creeks coming down the mountainsides from the solid masses of timber higher up. It is those fingers of cover the deer usually follow as they go up and down the mountains, avoiding broad openings.

With growing light we climbed a little faster, our labored breathing marked in puffs of steam, and we crossed a barbed-wire fence where we had made a stand another year. It was by that fence, my back to a rock outcropping, that I had listened to repeated twangings of the wire as unseen deer had crossed it before daylight, but on this later morning we went farther.

We separated to find individual stands. I bore to my left, the others went right. The going got choppier, with rocky patches and juniper clumps easy to see now. Behind me there were yellow specks of light in ranch windows. I reached a point where a shallow draw and its tiny iced creek deepened to a small, bushy canyon with tall timber a little farther up. I sat down on a rock, my outline broken by juniper and stone behind me. Back the way I had come there were scattered patches of timber, and just a little below me on the other side of the creek was a tongue of mature pines, separated from the creek by a wide park. My vision toward the valley was not perfect, but I counted on upward-bound game following the creek and coming within range.

I don't know how long the deer had been standing there. I had glanced about before sitting down and certainly I had been watching for movement, but suddenly he was there, a fat two-point buck, no more than 200 yards away across the draw, standing broadside and watching me. Most deer hunters have experienced the same thing and have wondered if the animal somehow arrived while they were watching somewhere else or if it had stood there for some time and been overlooked.

Deer season was almost over, it would be my last day's hunting, we could use the meat, and the rotund forkhorn certainly would satisfy Debie's kitchen requirements, so I slowly brought the rifle to position, slipped into the sling, and squirmed gently until the crosshairs hung steady behind the buck's shoulder. The shot boomed and rebounded in the canyon, and the deer seemed to have been erased as if he had been an imaginary deer after all. But when the muzzle came down after recoil I made out a gray horizontal form in the weeds where he had stood. The form did not move, so there was no hurry and a big buck might appear later. I faced a little more downhill, checking my first kill occasionally with binoculars, proud of my practical approach.

It was some time later that I first saw the big buck—I had almost concluded that all of the feeding deer had chosen routes that would not pass me. I first saw him as a dot far down toward the Madison as he appeared on a bit of high ground, and I barely focused the glasses before he was out of sight again. Some minutes later he appeared once more, much nearer, and I got a good view of sweeping antlers, thick neck and heavy shoulders. Even then it seemed likely he was heading for my draw, and I studied him whenever he was in view, moving steadily and deliberately up the slope, evidently returning from early feeding but also carrying the belligerent look of a harem seeker on the move. The rut was nearing its end and traveling bucks are common at that time of year, even the giants with little to fear from competitors.

It was some time before I began to estimate ranges. It was 600 yards, I thought, and then he was out of view again and I guessed 500 yards the next time he appeared, but he was coming closer and I started to look for the places where he might make a reasonable target—futile planning, for a deer seldom takes the route you lay out for him unless it is an established trail. He stopped to check the air at intervals as he neared the broken ground below the solid forest. It was broad daylight and he seemed to know he was a little late.

I swung my glasses over surrounding territory, fearful some other member of our party might appear on the slope without seeing the buck, but there was nothing to frighten him. I wondered about scent from me or the others, but he showed no apprehension and the air currents seemed favorable.

Then, after some steady upward progress on my side of the draw, the buck unaccountably turned to move at right angles to it and appeared about to cross. It was a long moment of decision, for there seemed little chance he would come closer. I still estimated he was more than 400 yards away, a hard choice for one who attempts to hold a personal rule of no shooting past 350. Until then I had remained calm enough, I thought, but the necessity for immediate choice brought my pulse up and the rifle was not quite steady when I sought a rest in a half-prone position against my rock. It was an automatic move, apparently a subconscious decision to shoot, even while I consciously debated with myself. With my hand finally on the rock and the forend on my hand the crosshairs went still and I told myself that only a wild trigger yank could spoil the shot now. I must hold over, I knew, and I put the crosshairs on the walking deer's dark-gray shoulder, then moved them up the distance I felt they should be, only to see he had reached the edge of the little creek and was about to cross. After the crossing there would be almost level ground, I thought, and he might stop for a look around, so I waited, my thumb checking the safety one more time.

He crossed the creek with a little hop of his front feet and pulled himself up on the level spot, where he came almost to a complete stop, and my finger began to tighten, the bold crosshairs dead steady.

I had not fired when the buck dropped away from my aiming point, falling forward, the great antlers still almost level as the head struck the ground, all in silence, and it seemed a long while before I heard someone else's shot and the bullet's thud. I put down the rifle to look for the gunner and finally saw two red specks far across the wide park and near the heavy timber from where Debie had shot her trophy buck. The other red speck was Mike Baker, and since my hunting season had ended, I started over to help them dress the kill. It was the best head we have ever taken.

As we came down the mountain with the two deer the sun gleamed on the thread of river in the valley, but it snowed again soon after that and the magical time between fall and winter was gone for another year.

Success
Without
Venison

ROBERT ELMAN

Hunting is one of the few joys in which experience usually turns out to be as exhilarating as the anticipation. And an equally deep satisfaction lies in the third phase—the looking back. After a while it becomes a separate skill. Proper reminiscing calls for an ability to soften the edges of remembered failures without blurring successes. The pure essence of an experience drifts into focus then, like the single most perfect frame in a movie film, a gleaming moment salvaged from time's rascally flow.

Each season enlarges my collection of trophy moments, major and minor. Once, after putting up a covey of quail, two friends and I were pocketing our birds when the pointer (not mine) bumped a single at a yardage that has sensibly lengthened with each recollection of the afternoon. I fired and the bird came down and a friend whose deft gunning I envy said; "Elman, that was rather a nice shot." That moment, a paltry trophy beside the Grand Slams and Big Fives of the elite, nonetheless dazzles me and confounds certain colleagues whose favorite amusement is watching me shoot. Then there was a morning spent almost in the shadow of a covered bridge in the lower Catskills, when the native woodcock seemed to be already gone and the flight birds not yet in. The colors of maples and alders and two sweetgum trees were such that at first I hadn't cared, but finally I was turning home in exasperation when a big dark grouse careened from somewhere behind me. For once my reflexes were fast enough.

The bridge, the maples, alders, sweetgums, the grouse—their colors remain with me, unaffected by the seasons. I recall as vividly the plunge of my first Canada goose out of an iron-gray sky on the Eastern Shore. It landed between stubble rows with a sound like a muffled drumbeat. I've known other moments of puzzling emotion while watching a springer circle ahead of an invisible ringneck to turn its sprint into a cackling flush, and again when I touched the hard, heavy antlers of a big mule deer I'd jumped from its bed one hot afternoon in Texas. Even in a collection as blithely unselective as mine, though, one trophy of remembrance overshadows the others and sustains a feeling of kinship with the game I've hunted. It concerns a deer I didn't kill. Perhaps the mounts on my walls hold more interest than a merely recollected head of game whose only remaining substance is in the memory. But I suspect there are other hunters who have a special feeling about game that, for one reason or another, they had to pass up.

The incident occurred a few miles from my Covered Bridge of the Grouse, along a procession of wooded ridges where I had tried for three days to kill a whitetail. I'd seen plenty of does, some of them trailed by big fawns, climbing the ridges in the early mornings. But the law decreed bucks only, and I hadn't seen so much as a spike. On the evening before, however, walking out of a hemlock swamp toward the road when it was getting too dark to shoot, I'd caught a glimpse of something bigger than any doe I'd seen there or elsewhere. It was just a glimpse—a blob of gray-black coming off a boulder-strewn slope below a sprawling beech flat. It melted into the dusky brush, materialized again for a split second, then vanished into the thick hemlock swamp.

I wanted to be back first thing in the morning, but at five a.m. the rain was coming down so hard my partner didn't want to go out. I knew he was right; unless the rain let up we wouldn't be able to see beyond fifteen or twenty yards. When it rains that hard on the beech ridges, every deer in that county seems to head for the strip of swamps. It's drier there under the hemlocks. "Darker, too," my partner observed ruefully. "It hurts to know where they are when there's no chance of seeing them."

For a couple of hours we listened to the rain rattling, watched it pelt the river, and stared at a sky washed in the glum color of our shared mood. Both of us had to be back at work the next day. By midmorning we talked about putting on rain pants and jackets, and to hell with visibility. Then, unexpectedly, the downpour began to abate. The sky lightened to pale silver as we started toward the swamp through the slapping, water-spattering brush. We had talked about still-hunting the slopes more or less together in the hope that one of us would push a deer toward the other. Either man just might get a shot if the other moved a buck a few hundred yards in a lucky direction. But he wanted to work the woods from the bottom, starting near the river and going slowly up through the hemlocks to the beech ridges. I had to admit it sounded sensible. The swamp usually held a few deer long after a hard rain. If it was late enough, they might be reluctant to go back up to the ridges at all; sometimes they stayed on the swampy lower slopes, among the huge sheltering hemlocks, until dusk drew them down to the fields and orchards. In the event of more rain, they'd probably move little if at all; and if the day got brighter there were sunny clearings among the hemlocks on the southwest slopes, warm and protected by a thick screen of woods.

All the same, I prefer to work down from above except very late in the day, and I was thinking about the big gray wraith I'd seen coming off the flat the previous evening. That deer had probably grown so large by staying alive longer than the deer sheltering in the hemlock swales near the river, near the road, where the local hunters habitually harvested their venison. I was trying to think (or calculate, or let my instincts guide me, or whatever the process may be) the way a shrewd old buck does. Maybe the deer I'd seen had gone to the swamp during the storm, but I felt sure he'd be back up on his sequestered beech flat now, on the other side of a razorback ridge, farther from the road than most hunters bothered to search. I had a notion he'd stay there until dusk.

After being rained out in the morning, I didn't have enough day left to try my partner's plan and my own as well, so we split up. He headed into the jungle of hemlocks and I skirted around and up, looking for a well-used deer run where the big shadowy animal had descended at dusk. There was a gentle saddle and a bench meandering down from the ridge to form a natural route for deer. I was betting I'd find the trail there.

I did, but I wasn't really prepared for what I saw. A muddy dip, about four yards long, passed beneath an overhang that formed a natural umbrella, and it was churned with tracks. Some of them hadn't yet filled with water. They'd probably been made after the rain, and they were large, very large. I saw no sign that a deer had bedded down here, nor did I notice any hair or find any buck rubs, but the place had been used hard and recently. It looked like a rutting wallow. The tracks were no dainty little split valentines characteristic of does and fawns. Most of them, sunk deeply and sharply into the mud, with raggedly round dewclaw marks behind the hooves, were broadly splayed at the front ends—perhaps two-thirds as wide as they were long. And they must have been well over three inches in length, closer to four with the trailing dewclaws. Even allowing for a deceptive spread in soft mud, those tracks had been left by a deer larger than most of the area's whitetails.

I moved to the right of the saddle and started up the slope, parallel to the deer trail, trying to stay in cover, going slowly, trying to climb quietly: a few steps and a pause rather than the steady pacing rhythm that deer recognize as human the moment they hear it. Determined to work hard at this last chance, to do everything right, I was thankful for the rain now. The ground carpet was soaked soft enough to make the going almost silent.

I reflected on another reason my partner so often favored

the swamp. Down there beneath the high black herringbone weave of needled branches were spreads of quilted moss, dark-green, light-green, yellow, deep and soft enough to muffle footsteps if a man watched for fallen twigs and boot-sucking mud seeps. Only powdery snow could baffle sound as well, and snow sometimes hid crackling branches. But even there, still-hunting as silently as some Iroquois ghost, it was easy to make mistakes. The previous year, I recalled, I'd been treading a moss quilt when I crunched a ravel of twigs and half a dozen flags exploded from a thicket like a bobwhite covey trading soybeans for honeysuckle.

Today I would be as well off on the wet carpeting of the beech flats, high, seldom hunted, sufficiently open in some places for eighty-yard shots. As I topped the ridge I paused for a careful look around, then picked up the game trail again and found copious droppings—pellets, acorn shapes, oblongs—their size more suggestive of elk than whitetail. My elation was of a calm new sort I hadn't known before. I was as well aware as anyone that the hunter never fully controls his situation, never can guarantee himself the sight of game, never conquers nature or wants to. Yet I was certain I'd find the deer—my deer—that had left those great splayed tracks and outsized scat. Looking back, I can see that my manic confidence was the optimism of the innocent. I felt I was working in harmony with nature, but nature is a fickle collaborator. Having read the sign and obeyed its messages, I indulged in the sure patience of a predator slowly closing with the game. I'd hunted within less than a mile of this spot in past years, but never had I felt so at home in the woods.

To the west the succession of ridges terminated at a granite promontory, known locally as the Catbird Seat, above a valley thinly veiled with oaks, beeches, and other hardwoods. I'd gone on stand there when the valley funneled deer from their beds to their favorite lowland feeding grounds. Even the cautious bucks seldom appeared to expect danger from above, and the view was splendid from the Catbird Seat. But it had been heavily hunted this year, and by the time I'd arrived the deer were skirting the valley, moving up soon after daybreak by way of the side slopes. In two days I'd seen only a single small doe down there and I was glad now to be farther in and up, combing the whitetail's highest possible retreat.

Hunting upwind of the game trail, I spotted a huge, head-high, flat-topped boulder. By God, I'd found my own private Catbird Seat, overlooking thinly wooded flats that dipped gently away toward the side slopes of the valley. Less than forty yards off, a stretch of the deer run was furrowed with use, beaten to a clear path. I'd come quite a distance from the river road. Since visitors who drove up from the city seldom penetrated deeper than half a mile from their parked cars, it wasn't likely there had been much hunting pressure here.

The afternoon was ebbing. If the big half-seen deer of the previous evening habitually kept to the same trails, my quarry would have to pass this way before long. I checked the safety and raised the rifle to scan the flats, mentally remarking that a 2½-power scope would serve me better up here than down in the hemlock swamp. Then, with nothing left to do, I happily sat on my rock and listened to the woods. Half an hour passed, and nearly another half an hour. The day had been warm for a while after the rain, but now the temperature was sinking. Chilled dejection slowly began to displace the glow of overconfidence I'd felt when I topped the ridge. The wind shifted, blowing straight from me to the game trail. I lit a cigarette. To hell with it.

I don't recall how I spotted the deer. I saw it before I heard anything, and at first I had no idea I was looking at an animal. It was a patch of gray between thick beech trunks of the same color. A low, scrawny sprig jutted from one of the trunks like the bones of a hand, with tan leaves dangling from its skeletal fingers. Perhaps the deer moved as I looked that way, or the breeze fluttered the withered leaves and exposed some little contour of gray that couldn't be a tree. For all I know the deer could have been standing there for many minutes or it might have come along the trail seconds ago. Now it ambled back through a little thicket and around some boulders, apparently headed away from me. As I kept watching, the gray shape approached again, but showed only patches of flank through the trees and brush. Though I could tell it was big, the planes of its body were shattered by the screening vegetation into unrecognizable shards of movement.

Finally it stepped partway into a low opening. I wondered if my hands were steady. The deer was stretching its neck, nibbling at twigs, its head veiled behind the browse, and I couldn't tell whether I was seeing thick antler tines or thin tree limbs.

But I could see that the animal must have stood almost four feet high at the shoulder, and the back of a New York whitetail doesn't come up to a man's chest. The legs were as thick as heavy saplings, and I could even make out one forefoot. For a gambling second I put the scope there, on the foot, trying to confirm that this animal had left the big splayed prints I'd found. I couldn't tell, of course. Still, the cloven hoof seemed exceptionally large.

I shifted my hold way up, straining to see more of the head, when the deer stepped forward again. There were no antlers. I couldn't believe it. Does weighing 170 or 180 pounds simply didn't exist in this part of the country. Even now I like to tell myself I was seeing an antlerless buck, an aged male that had lost the mysterious hormonal life forces needed to produce antler growth. It happens sometimes to very old bucks. But doe or buck, it was bald, and wishing would not soften the game laws.

A kill is sometimes the least important part of hunting, but I'm a stranger to the company of saints. I studied that head for a long time, wanting desperately to see headgear of any sort, even barely legal spikes. I let myself think for a second or two about how I might explain things if I chanced to meet a warden: how easy it is, after all, to mistake tree limbs for a buck's rack. Yet it wasn't the thought of a heavy fine that stopped me, nor the twinge of shame at the idea of violating a code I claimed to uphold.

It was a sudden realization—or just a gratifying notion maybe—that I'd already succeeded on this hunt. My satisfaction stood there, an antlerless prank of nature but proof enough for me that I'd thought (or calculated, or let my instincts guide me, or whatever) like a deer; I'd read the sign and obeyed its messages, I'd found the deer I had set out to find. I needed only a final gesture to slake the ego of my hunting drive—the atavistic drive all hunters feel to discover whether they can secure the meat of the woods as their progenitors did in some dim, wild past. I checked to make sure I hadn't unconsciously slipped the safety off, then put the crosshairs on the animal's brisket as it turned to face me, squeezed the trigger slowly, and grinned at the silence.

Some moments of truth last longer than a moment. The deer came within thirty yards of me, unaware of my existence as its head tilted to nibble twigs at the browse line and occasionally bowed to pick a morsel from the mast at its feet. I watched, feeling a strengthening kinship with this animal that I loved and wanted to kill. As the deer finally vanished beneath a shadowy understory of beech saplings, I recalled a story my friend Joe Martin once told me during a Texas turkey hunt.

An old man had asked Joe to guide him on his last deer hunt, and had mentioned that his wife would come along as she used to years ago. Frail and palsied, the old man was probably right to believe this would be his last hunt, but little exertion was needed, for they sought a good buck by cruising the arid brush country in a ranch car. Deer were plentiful, the rut was at its peak, chances were good. A little after daybreak, when they had driven only a couple of miles, Joe spotted something at the edge of a mesquite thicket. A brief stalk revealed a sight rarely witnessed—a buck mounting a doe. The animals seemed oblivious of intrusion as the old man approached, with his wife and Joe close behind. The old man put the crosshairs on the buck's spine but he didn't fire. His wife gently touched his shoulder. Lowering the rifle, he grinned, took her hand, and walked back to the car. Late that afternoon he took a fat eight-pointer. But I think he had already savored a keener moment of hunting truth that morning, as I savored mine while I watched my deer—a doe perhaps but an aged buck to me—vanish into the woods.

The Sundown Covey

LAMAR UNDERWOOD

Nobody ever used that name, really. But it was the covey of bob-white quail that we always looked for, almost with longing, as we turned our hunt homeward in the afternoon. By the time we came to that last stretch of ragged corn and soybean fields where this covey lived, the pines and moss-draped oaks would be looming darkly in the face of the dying sun. The other events of the afternoon never seemed to matter then. Tired pointer dogs bore ahead with new drive; we would watch carefully as they checked out each birdy objective, sure that we were headed for a significant encounter before we reached the small lane that led to the Georgia farmhouse. I always chose to think of those birds as "the sundown covey," although my grandfather or uncle usually would say something like "Let's look in on that bunch at the end of the lane." And then, more times than not, the evening stillness would be broken by my elder's announcement, "Yonder they are!" and we would move toward the dogs on point—small stark-white figures that always seemed to be chiseled out of the shadowy backdrop against the evening swamp.

There's always something special about hunting a covey of quail that you know like an old friend. One covey's pattern of movements between fields and swampy sanctuaries can be an intriguing and baffling problem. Another may be remarkably easy to find, and yet always manage to rocket away through such a thick tangle that you've mentally colored them *gone,* even before your finger touches the trigger. Another might usually present a good covey shot, while the singles tear away to . . . the backside of the moon, as far as you've been able to tell. My best hunts on more distant but greener pastures somehow have never seemed as inwardly satisfying as a day when a good dog and I can spend some time on familiar problems like these. Give me a covey I know, one that has tricked me, baffled me, eluded me—and by doing so brought me back to its corner of the woods for years.

In this sense, the covey we always hunted at sundown was even more special. As the nearest bunch of birds to the house, it was the most familiar. Here, trembling puppies got onto their first points. A lad learned that two quick shots into the brownish blur of the covey rise would put nothing into his stiff new hunting coat. A man returning from a war saw the birds running quick-footed across the lane and knew that he really was home again. The generations rolled on through times of kerosene lamps and cheap cotton to Ed Sullivan and soil-bank subsidies. And that same covey of bobwhites that had always seemed a part of the landscape still whistled in the long summer afternoons and hurtled across dead cornstalks that rattled in the winter breezes.

The hunters who looked for that covey and others in the fields nearby disciplined themselves never to shoot a covey below six birds. That number left plenty of seed for replenishment, so that every fall the coveys would again number fifteen to thirty birds, depending on how they had fared against predators.

Eventually, all that acreage moved out of our family. My visits to those coveys became less frequent as I necessarily turned toward education and then fields of commerce that were far away. But even during some marvelous quail-hunting days in other places, I often longed for return hunts to those intriguing coveys of the past. Would the swamp covey by the old pond still be up to their usual trick of flying into the field in the afternoon? Where would the singles from the peafield covey go now? Would the sundown covey still be there?

Finally, not long ago, the opportunity came for me to knock about a bit down in the home county. Several hunts with friends seemed as mere preludes to the long-awaited day when I got a chance to slip away alone to the old home grounds.

A soft rain had fallen during the night, but when I parked the truck by a thicket of pines just after sunrise, a stiff breeze had started tearing the overcast apart, and patches of blue were showing through the dullness. Shrugging into my bird vest, I ignored the shufflings and impatient whines that sounded from the dog box and stood a moment looking across a long soybean field that stretched toward a distant line of pines. I was mentally planning a route that would take me in a big circle to a dozen or so familiar coveys, then bring me to the sundown covey in the late evening. I unlatched the dog box, and the pointer, Mack, exploded from the truck and went through a routine of nervous preliminaries. I did the same, checking my bulging coat for shells, lunch and coffee. Then I clicked the double shut and stepped into the sedge alongside the field, calling: "All right, Mack. Look around!"

The pointer loped away in that deceptive, ground-eating gait that was his way of going. At age four, he had not exactly developed into the close worker I had been wanting. His predecessors who had run these fields in decades before were big-going speedsters suited to those times. Controlled burning and wide-roaming livestock kept the woodlands open then. Now most of the forests were so choked with brush and vines that wide-working dogs brought a legacy of frustration. Mack was easy to handle but tended to bend out too far from the gun unless checked back frequently. I really hated hearing myself say

"Hunt close!" so often, but I hated even worse those agonizing slogging searches when he went on point in some dark corner of the swamp a quarter-mile from where I thought he'd been working.

The sun was bright on the sedge and pines now, and the air winy-crisp after the rain. Mack was a bouncing flash of white as he worked through the sedge and low pines. Once he started over the fence into the field, but I called him back. I wanted him to keep working down the edge. While the bean field seemed a tempting place to catch a breakfasting bevy, the cover bordering it offered much better chances—at least three to one, according to the quail-hunting education I had received here as a youngster. I could still imagine the sound of my grandfather's voice as he preached:

"Never mind all them picturebook covey rises in those magazines you read. It's only now and then you'll catch these old woods coveys in the open. Birds once had to range wide and root hard for their keep. Now all the work's done for 'em. Combines and cornpickers leave so much feed scattered in the field the birds can feed in a few minutes, then leg it back into the cover. That's where you want to work. First, if they haven't gone to feed, you're likely to find 'em. If they've walked into the field, the dog'll trail 'em out. If they've already been into the field and fed, you'll still find 'em. Only time you'll miss is when they've flown into the field and are still there."

I had seen this simple philosophy pay increasing dividends as the years wore on. As the cover became thicker and the coveys smarter, the clear covey shot had become a rare, treasured experience. To spend a lot of time working through the fields was to be a dreamer of the highest order.

Still in the cover, we rounded the end of the small field and headed up the other side. I was beginning to feel the bite of the day's first disappointment; Mack had picked up no scent at all. Where were they? This covey had always been easy to find. Maybe they had been shot out, I thought. Maybe the whole place has been shot out.

I decided to play out a hunch. I pulled down a rusty strand of fence and stepped out into the field. Mack leaped the wire and raced away at full gallop. Far downfield he turned into the wind and suddenly froze in one of the most dramatic points I've ever seen. I knew he was right on top of those birds, his body curved tautly, his tail arching. "Oh ho!" I said aloud. "So you beggars *did* fly to the field."

My strides lengthened and became hurried. I snapped the gun open and checked the shells in an unnecessary gesture of nervousness. Normally steady hands seemed to tremble a little and felt very thick and uncertain. My heartbeat was a thunderous throb at the base of my throat.

My tangled nerves and wire-taut reflexes scarcely felt the nudge of a thought that said, "Relax. You've done this before." The case of shakes I undergo every time I step up to a point makes it difficult to attach any importance to that idea. Covey-rise jitters are known to have only one cure: action.

On my next step, the earth seemed to explode. The air was suddenly filled with blurry bits and pieces of speeding fragments, all boring toward the pines that loomed ahead. I found myself looking at one particular whirring form, and when the stock smacked against my face, the gun bucked angrily. The brown missile was unimpressed. He faded into the swamp, along with a skyful of surviving kinsmen. My loosely poked second shot failed to drop a tail-ender.

Mighty sorry gathering up of partridges, I thought, using the expression that was my uncle's favorite on the occasions when we struck out on a covey rise. "Sorry, boy," I called to Mack, who was busy vacuuming the grass in a futile search for downed birds.

My elders would have thought that bevy's maneuver of flying out to the field was the lowest trick in the book. But now the practice had become so typical among smart southern Bobs that it was hardly worth lamenting.

I called Mack away from his unrewarding retrieve and headed after those singles. The woods ahead looked clear enough for some choice shooting if I could keep Mack close.

Thirty minutes later I emerged from those woods a frustrated, angry man. My estimate that the birds had landed in the grassy, open pinelands was about two hundred yards wrong. Instead they had sailed on into one of the thickest, darkest sweet-gum swamps I've ever cursed a bird dog in. It took Mack all of fifteen seconds to get lost, and when I found him on point after ten minutes of searching I proceeded to put the first barrel into a gum tree and the second into a screen of titi bushes. Then the heebie-geebies really took over as I walked over two separate singles that jumped unannounced. Finally, Mack pointed again, but as I fought through the tearing clutches of briers and vines to get to him, I bumped another single, which I shot at without a glimmer of hope. That action caused Mack to take matters into his own hands and send the bird he was pointing vaulting away through the trees. Then followed a lot of unnecessary yelling, and we headed for the clear.

I should have known better. Single-bird hunting in that part of Georgia had become a sad business. Now I was discovering that my old hunting grounds were in the same shape as the rest of the county. If you were going to mess with singles, you had to wait for the right type of open woods. Most were just too thick to see a dog, much less a six-ounce bird. The day's shooting was certainly not going to follow the patterns of the past when it came to singles. I would have to wait until I got a bevy scattered in a better place.

We cut away from the field into a section of low moss-draped oak trees. Mack ranged ahead, working smartly. My frustrations of the first covey slipped away as I began considering the coming encounter with the next set of old friends. This covey, if they were still in business, would be composed of dark swamp birds that lived in the edge of the creek swamp but used this oak ridge to feed on acorns during early mornings and late afternoons. They were extremely hard to catch in the open, sometimes running for hundreds of yards in front of a dog on point. But what a sight they always made as they hurtled up among the moss-draped oaks on the lucky occasions when we did get them pinned nicely.

This oak ridge was fairly open, so I let Mack move on out a little bit. When he cut through one thickish cluster of trees and did not come out right away, I knew he had 'em.

Incredible, I thought. *The first two coveys are still here, and we've worked 'em both.* Then the words turned into brass in my mouth as I eased up to the dog and past him. The thunderous rise I had been expecting failed to occur. I let Mack move on ahead to relocate. Catlike, he crept through the low grass for a few yards, then froze again. I moved out in front once more, and still nothing happened.

Then, suddenly I heard them. Several yards out front the

dry leaves rustled under the flow of quick-moving feet. The covey was up to its old trick of legging it for the sanctuary of the swamp.

I hurried forward, crashing through the briars. Just ahead, the low cover gave way to a wall of sweetgum and cypress that marked the beginning of the swamp. Too late! I caught the sound of wings whirring. The birds had made the edge and were roaring off through the trees. They seemed to get up in groups of two and three. I caught an occasional glimpse of dim blurs through the screen of limbs and snapped a shot at one. Leaves and sticks showered down as Mack raced forward. Seconds later he emerged from the brush carrying a plump rooster bobwhite.

Had you seen me grinning over that bird, you might have thought I hadn't scored in five years. But the shot seemed mighty satisfying under the conditions. A few moments like this could make the day a lot more glorious than a coatful of birds ever could.

Now we followed an old lane that led down across the swamp and out beside a tremendous cornfield surrounded by pine and gallberry flats. I expected to find a couple of coveys here—and did, too, as the morning wore on in a succession of encounters with my old friends. A heart-warming double from a bevy Mack pinned along a fence row was followed by a succession of bewildering misses when we followed the singles into an open gallberry flat where I should have been able to score. Then we had the fun of unraveling a particularly difficult relocation problem when Mack picked up some hot scent in the corn but could not trail out to the birds. The edge of the field sloped down a grassy flat to an old pond with pine timber on the far side. I just knew those birds had flown across that pond to the woods to hole up for the day. When I took Mack over he made a beautiful point, standing just inside the woods. I wish I could always dope out a covey like that.

We spent the middle of the day stretched out on the grass on the pond dam. The sandwiches and coffee couldn't have tasted better. The sun was warm, and crows and doves flew against the blue sky. I thought about old hunts and old friends and couldn't have felt better.

In the afternoon we had a couple of interesting pieces of action, but failed to find some of my old neighbor coveys at home. My thoughts kept reaching ahead to the late-afternoon time when I would near the old now-deserted house by the lane and see the sundown covey again. Surely they would still be there. After all, we had been finding most of the old coveys. Who says you can't go home again? Who's afraid of you, Tom Wolfe?

The sun was dipping toward the pines and a sharp chill had come on when I skirted the last field and entered a stretch of open pine woods where I was counting on finding the covey of birds that I had carried in my mind all my life. Before I had gone fifty yards I came on something that shocked me as though I'd walked up on a ten-foot rattlesnake. A newly cut stake had been driven in the ground, and a red ribbon tied to the top of it. Farther on there was another, then another.

I had known that the new Savannah-Atlanta-Super-High-Speed-Interstate-Get-You-There-Quick-Highway was to pass through this general area. But surely, a couple of miles away. Not here. Not right here.

Gradually, my disbelief turned into anger. I felt like heading for the car right then and getting the hell out of there. Then suddenly three shots boomed in the woods some distance ahead.

Well, it was apparent that the sundown covey was still around. But an intruder had found them. I decided to go on up and talk to whoever it was. Actually, he probably had as much right to be here as I did now. I couldn't believe he was a regular hunter on this land, though. The coveys I had been finding all day were too populous with birds to be gunned heavily.

I walked slowly through the pines for a few minutes without spotting the other hunter. Then his gun thudded again, this time from farther down in the swamp. He's after the singles now, I thought. I called in Mack and waited there opposite the swamp. The other fellow would have to come out this way.

During the next few minutes two more separate shots sounded. The sun sank lower, and the breeze blew harder in the pines. Finally, I heard the bushes shaking and a man came out of the cover. When Mack started barking he spotted me and headed my way. As he came up I saw that he was young, carried an automatic and wore no hunting coat. He had some quail by the legs in his left hand.

"Looks like you did some good," I said.

"Yea, I got six."

"Where's your dog?" I asked.

"Oh, I don't have a dog. I spotted a covey crossing the road

down there by the lane. I had the gun in the truck, so I went after 'em. Got three when I flushed 'em and three more down in
the branch. Tiny little covey, though. I don't think there were
more than six when I first flushed 'em. I imagine people been
framin' into this bunch all the time." My heart sank when he
said that. I didn't know what to say. He paused a minute, looking at Mack. "That's a nice dog. He any good?"

"Fair," I said. "Maybe you shouldn't have done that."

"What?"

"Shoot a small covey on down that way."

"Don't mean nothing. There's always a covey of birds along
here. Every year. But there won't be for long. Interstate's coming through."

"Yea," I said slowly. "I see it is."

"Well, I gotta run. That's sure a nice-looking dog, Mister.
See you around."

I watched him walk away. Then I leaned back against a
pine, listening to the swamp noises. The wings of a pair of roost-
bound ducks whispered overhead. An owl tuned up down in the
swamp. Somehow I kept thinking that I would hear some birds
calling each other back into a covey. Perhaps two or three had
slipped away unseen from the roadside.

The night pressed down. Trembling in the cold, I started
for the truck. Orion wheeled overhead. I started thinking about
some new places I wanted to try. But never again did I hear that
flutelike call that had sounded for me from that swamp so many
times before.

Pepper

GENE HILL

No one I ever knew ever admitted, in those late gray hours when the fire wants you to leave it alone so it can go out, to owning the best gun he ever saw, the best dog he ever saw or the prettiest woman he ever saw. At least nobody I know.

I shot the best gun I ever saw—one time. It was a single-barrel A. H. Fox, from Philadelphia. The man who owned it bought it for one hundred and fifty dollars and added it to his collection of over eighty fine trap guns. As far as I know he shot it only once ever, the day he let me take it out for fifty targets—

and each and every one I smoked right in the middle. I saw him a few times after that and offered him what I could, pitiful amounts, really, and all he ever did was smile. I guess I'm just as glad in a way that I never did get my hands on that old Fox for keeps . . . owning something has a way of putting tarnish on the dream. Owning anything does, maybe. I'm not sure, but I think maybe it does.

I know a few men who do very well in the eyes of their accountants, and most of them are the same as us in the long run. Same little problems that men have because they're only men. Nature and time never single out "rich" men. They just deal with men, and we all sort of get the same hand dealt to play—and as the cards are turned over the same things show every time—sooner or later.

You might get dealt "my" old Fox, for example, and have that followed up by a nasty flinch or a failing eye. I hope not, of course; I'm just doing that for example so you'd know what I meant. No fancy philosophy, just a simple way of looking at fate and what passes for justice as far as I know; the kind of thing we always are reading about in the evening paper. Things that happen in South Dakota or Mississippi, except sometimes it's somebody we know real well. Sometimes it's us.

It always seemed to me, the times I get to thinking about such things, that nobody I ever know gets his name in the paper or even passed around town in the post office for anything especially good. I mean really good. You know—the sort of thing that'll make a man in his middle years sleep differently than most of us, without that little cloud sitting right there in front of tomorrow or in front of the day or week after.

It's not that I care that much about having the best things of anything. I don't think I'd always know the best if I saw it, but sometimes you figure you'd like to know what it would be like. I admit I'd like to get my hands on a Purdey for a season at quail . . . not to own forever because I'd get to worrying about it, but just a time long enough to know if I'd been really missing something important all my life—not that I could do anything about it, but just to know. The way I'd like to drive a Rolls-Royce with all that smell of wood and leather and elegance floating around me. I'd even like to go into a store, one time, and feel that the coat I was trying on had never been on anyone else ever before; instead of always feeling that someone else has seen it and didn't like it, had felt the cloth and didn't feel it was up to their wants. I don't mean to go putting on airs, but it doesn't do any harm to sort of skylark in your mind about something as long as it doesn't cost anything or do anybody any harm. I never wanted anything that really belonged to anybody else, either. At least not in the sense of taking something away they'd feel hurt about bad. The old A. H. Fox didn't mean much to the man that owned it . . . it just meant a lot to me. I really feel, even now, that somehow that old single-barrel meant more to me than anyone. Or ever had. It's just a feeling; doesn't mean much. But there it is. Because I really liked that gun. I liked it past the point of being able to shoot it real well, if you follow me. Just a funny thing, but here it's stayed with me for so long.

I never really envied anybody very much, and the way I feel about the old gun isn't envy as much as it is something private and selfish. I guess it's a feeling of waste. The way you feel when you know a fine woman and know her husband drinks too much or something like that. I get along pretty good with what I've got. I don't have much time or use for complaining. It never does much good as far as I can see. Complaining about the rocks never got the well dug. I never cared much about being the best shot around, or gunning the biggest bag either. I manage to take my share in fair sport and I think I enjoy it as much as most and sometimes more. But if I could do it all over and have just one small wish, I'd be tempted to ask whoever it is you ask to give me a dog like Pepper.

I said that I never knew of a man admitting to owning the best dog he ever saw, and I mean it. Because the man that owned Pepper was one of the few men on God's green earth that I really didn't like. Not that I like everybody I have to come in contact with by a long shot, but I have my own feeling about what's right and wrong, even if a man only does it once.

Pepper was a small dog compared to your big-going pointers and a fair-sized dog compared to your English setters. I believe he was about half and half, and if he could or cared to, Pepper might admit to a touch of the German shorthair. Yet, somehow, in him it all came together just right. Except for being maybe a little too dark, he was sort of a very light gray, dapple, you might put it. But that sort of suited me too, because that's the color Pepper should have been, if you follow me. It was his

particular color by nature. He wasn't either bold or shy. And you weren't ever conscious of him being around the way you are about some dogs. When he was wanted he just sort of materialized out of a corner, or drifted in from the barn or appeared in the back of the pickup truck. And that was the way he hunted for partridge and woodcock. You'd sort of be wondering where he was and wasn't that a likely spot over there by the thorn apples and sure enough, there'd be old Pepper working the softest wind just right.

Pepper had the kind of walk that always tickled me. I tried a thousand times to describe it, but the only word I know that comes close is "tentative." He sort of walked as if he questioned everything, a little hitching step that had a purpose but not a total commitment to that direction he seemed to be going in. He sort of just drifted along; you always felt he knew what he was doing, but that he was prepared to change his mind if a really good reason came along. He walked like a dog who has more than a little sense of humor, in a philosophical way.

I always felt I could ask Pepper to do great things, undoglike things, and he would, if he could ever have understood me, but for the time being he was content to do our bird work for us, since it pleased us, or at least me, mightily, and it was so incredibly, so consummately easy for him to be perfect at it.

To my certain knowledge, Pepper never had one minute of any kind of training, and less than that of kindness or affection from the man that kept him. Yet I never saw him break at shot; he would often, if you missed a woodcock or grouse, sort of step to one side so he could more clearly mark the bird down. If a bird fell in water or across a brook or pond, Pepper would take to the water gently, like an old man going in inch by inch, but he never flagged at it, skim ice or none. He often half climbed a tree to fetch a bird lodged in a branch; he'd dig a pheasant out of a hole and work as hard as his strength allowed to get after a bird in a stone wall.

One of the things I most enjoyed about Pepper was the variety of styles on point. He did everything on a bird but your traditional stiff-legged, ramrod-tail stand. Often he'd just be there and sort of nod his head in the direction of the bird. Sometimes he'd sit if he had to wait any length of time for you to come up, and several times, especially in a field with low grass cover, he'd actually lie down, stretched out straight like a rug, and often the bird would be as far in front of him as fifty or sixty yards.

He had an incredible desire to conserve his strength, and Lord knows he should have, the way we worked him, but I never saw him really tired out. One habit that I always took pleasure in was the way he'd lean on things. If you were just standing around talking, Pepper would lean on your leg, or a nearby tree or against the car wheels. He never bounded out until everyone else was completely ready, then he'd rouse himself and go off to work after a small survey of the cover to see which spot made the most sense.

The man that owned Pepper was one of those strange beings who don't like animals. He didn't like Pepper any more than he liked his hay rake or tractor. Pepper was a thing he used to hunt birds. No more, no less.

He fed and cared for the dog with the same thoroughness he cared for any machine that needed fuel and oil and water. And that's just the way he used him—when the season closed Pepper was on his own. Where he lived or wandered was no concern to his owner. When the season was open Pepper stayed around living in the barn when it was cold and sleeping in the back of the pickup truck on a feed sack when it wasn't.

I believe that the man that owned Pepper hunted for only a couple of reasons, none of them having the slightest bearing on what we would call "sporting instincts." One reason was that he was as near a perfect field shot as I have ever seen. To my knowledge he never picked up a shotgun between seasons, never shot a single clay target. As much as I felt a coolness or more between us I'd have bet my mortgage on him in a live pigeon match against anyone. In fact I'd bet on him against anyone at any game that involved a shotgun, giving him a few minutes to study what the game was. He wasn't an especially fast shot. By that I mean he didn't pull up his gun and fire in a blur of speed. He had his gun up fast enough all right, because he'd never even consider my getting a shot in turn, if and when he knew he could kill a bird he shot—whether it was on your side or not. He expected you to do the same with him, in all fairness. And he never shot at a bird he wasn't very sure of hitting and he took what I consider a helluva lot of tough shots—at least tough to me. He had an uncanny sense of distance, unlike most bird hunters who think so many birds are too far and don't shoot.

He knew his gun—a low-grade Parker 16-gauge—would take a fair shot at a grouse at nearly fifty yards, and he killed a good many that I just stood and stared at—and a good many more that I'd shot at and missed.

I'm not sure now that he really did take a great deal of pride, or any, in his ability with a shotgun or really thought much of it. I believe he was one of those rare men who were just born that way and he never knew it could be any other way—or cared. That old VH Parker was just a tool that he knew how to use; like a double-bitted ax is to an expert lumberman.

He hunted to shoot birds to eat—and that was that. I've always thought it was a good thing he was a hard-working farmer instead of a hunting fanatic, because without thinking about it, and he wouldn't have, he could have very easily reduced the local bird population to near zero.

That's the only reason I got to hunt so much with Pepper—he had to do chores and I'd come by and pick Pepper up. If he wasn't busy, though, he would throw his gun in the car and come along.

We never had much to say to each other—in fact there'd be quite a few times when we literally never spoke beyond some common salutation. I'd soon quit saying "nice shot" or whatever nicety came to mind when he made one of his many spectacular kills since it seemed to bore or even annoy him. In time our mutual silence got to be rather pleasant to me, since I could spend more and more time observing and sort of chatting to old Pepper—who in all honesty didn't pay much attention to either one of us. He was a free spirit, all down the line.

The three of us hunted—each in a world of his own, and still together. A strange and different motive for each one of us, yet tied together in our rather odd contract. If it hadn't been that I knew most of the decent covers and had once asked him along to hunt on his farm I still wonder if we'd have ever gotten together at all.

The year before last was the final time I ever saw either one of them. We'd hunted the end day of the season and it seemed as if Pepper was putting on a special show for me. As usual he was flawless, something I'd come to expect by now. His points on the three grouse I picked up were typical—one where he sat and nodded toward a patch of scrub oak, another where I found him leaning against a small birch, his head turned around the bole of the tree, like a man scratching his neck, and the third where I saw him just standing there as if he were half asleep.

As usual I was outgunned two to one and as usual no one spoke, except for my ordinary chit-chat with Pepper, who as usual, took no notice of it.

I let them out at the gate to the farm and something made me sit there and wait and watch them walk back toward the barn. My blue-overalled companion never once looked back, nor did my adored Pepper. Side by side they walked until the man turned away from the barn path toward the house. Pepper hesitated a moment, then turned from the other path that led to the barn and began again to follow the man. Then the man stopped, and without a single word kicked Pepper in the shoulder hard enough to roll him over. The dog picked himself up and turned around and disappeared into the barn.

I've always regretted to the point of being sick of myself that I didn't follow my instincts and go, right then, and ask if I could have that dog. It was as if I'd suffered some unimaginable cruelty to myself and been afraid to cry out, found something in me that I didn't really know was there, and I despised that thing in me that I will have to live with forever—that act of cowardice that allowed or forced me to merely drive away.

I drove by the farm often that summer, each time with a recurrence of a feeling of fear and dread. Each time I was firmly resolved to stop in and ask for Pepper, offer money for the dog and have an end to my nightmare. But somehow I never did. I like to think it was because I never saw the man close up, only a distant figure on a tractor in a field or so away. But I know that's not the truth.

I know now that the truth lay in my subconscious. The knowledge that some things are not ever to be. There are things to be admired but never owned. There are things to be seen but never to become a part of us. Shadows that fall across some part of our lives.

I never stopped at the farm that fall, and even went out of my way not to drive by. But even now, as I hunt alone, I often stop and wait and listen knowing that it's only a cruel trick of my imagination that I see a dappled brown-eyed dog leaning against the far side of a birch tree staring around it at me with patient expectation as if he'd been there waiting all along for me, and me alone, to come by.

Epilogue

JIM RIKHOFF

Someone once said the killing of an animal during a hunt is really anticlimatic, and certainly it is a time of paradox—regret mixed with triumph. There is a curious post-hunting depression that usually evolves into a sustained elation. Lastly, there is the quiet satisfaction in a job well done and a trophy well taken—if one has played the game as rules, both written and unwritten, tell us it should be played. This is the time of reflection, of remembrances of experiences shared, of victories and defeats—equally rewarding as viewed through the prism of time.

What about all that time between the planning of a hunt and the so-called moment of truth—the trigger-pulling, if you will—and what about the period after the kill before the trip is over? Well, I can tell you a big-game hunt is a mixed bag indeed—some fun, a little misery, a lot of hard work, but all rewarding. Anyone who has ever packed into the high country or struggled through the almost obscene undergrowth of jungle lowlands or drifted across a heat-stricken midday desert knows that one pays for one's trophies in many coins. I have hung, exhausted and bone-weary, on the side of a mountain while a driving, freezing rain pounded its way through every dry crevice of my clothing and wondered why I—who fear heights and despise being wet and cold—am at that particular spot at that specific time.

The answer is simple. I am there because I want to be there—not for that miserable experience, but for the possible moment that *may be* before that trip is done. I may not even know what that moment will be—one of "truth" or not—but I search for it, drive myself toward it, and am irresistibly drawn toward it. In the last analysis, I not only want to be there—hanging on the side of that mountain, wandering across that desert or slogging through that jungle—but, if the truth were to be admitted, I probably need to be there too. And in that, perhaps, we have the real meaning of the "moment of truth" as it applies to hunters, if not all men. We are hunters hunting because that is what we are supposed to do, have always done, and—hopefully—will always try to do in the future. I am reminded of Theodore Roosevelt's fine words that describe hunting much better than my attempts:

> No one but he who has partaken thereof, can understand the keen delight of hunting in lonely lands. For him is the joy of the horse well ridden and the rifle well held; for him the long days of toil and hardship, resolutely endured, and crowned at the end with triumph. In after-years there shall come forever to his mind the memory of endless prairies shimmering in the bright sun; of vast snow-clad wastes lying desolate under gray skies; of the melancholy marshes; of the rush of mighty rivers; of the breath of the evergreen forest in summer; of the crooning of ice-armored pines

at the touch of the winds of winter; of cataracts roaring between hoary mountain masses; of all the innumerable sights and sounds of the wilderness; of its immensity and mystery; and of the silences that brood in its still depths.

It has always amazed me when those opposed to hunting have condemned the practice as unholy, immoral and alien to man's finer purposes. What utter disregard of all the facts of history, folklore, and natural history, and the overwhelming evidence of life and death about us! What complete poppycock! The only thing unholy, immoral and alien to man and all nature is that which is simply unnatural—false, contrived, artificial, forced, constricted and twisted against nature's innate systems and balances. Since man is a hunter by nature, the act of hunting can hardly be an "unnatural" act, let alone immoral, unethical or unholy. There are those who rather desperately attempt to deny man is a hunter, but I would consign them to argument with more qualified men than I—namely, the overwhelming majority of anthropologists.

When man is denied his hunting instincts and the natural aggressive drives that have preserved this rather puny animal down through the centuries, he often finds himself in very deep trouble. On the one hand, man becomes weakened as he is frustrated in his instincts, his society softens, and his civilization wastes away in the face of stronger challenges. On an individual basis, certain men channel their thwarted aggression into antisocial behavior: ruthless business practice, predatory sexual conquest and even criminal action, either through personal assault or in collective war.

Certain self-appointed voices of so-called modern civilized thought decry hunting as an outmoded, discredited and incompatible pastime in modern society. These seers—usually urban-bred and -based—abhor the country sports as, indeed, they really fear the country. They hope to conquer by ridicule and involuted logic the strength of the countryside, its mores and morality, its basic standards and its very validity.

When our critics condemn hunting as uncivilized, they ignore the historical fact that hunting was the catalyst of man's coming together in any form of organized society in the first place. They ignore the fact that hunting provided both the backdrop and the impetus to our first art forms—from cave paintings, to lyric songs and dances celebrating the chase, to panoramic tapestries on castle walls, to epic poems singing the praises of Odysseus and Beowulf. Lastly, they ignore the facts of human life: man is a predator, perhaps the most efficient and magnificent predator the world has ever seen.

The love of hunting is nothing to instill shame in the human race. It was once popular to condemn all predation, but now at least we have come to recognize and admire the necessary role of the predator in the lower forms of animal life. The eagle is now protected—well, almost protected—throughout the land, and the hawks and falcons are coming into their own, although a little late for the saving in some instances. The great cats—many of them endangered species—are wondered over and looked upon as symbols of grace, power and authority over the world. Paradoxically, it has been the hunter who has led the battle for the protection of his fellow predators in many cases.

Consequently, predator and predation are no longer "scare" words in the classic sense with the general populace. Predatory animals and their importance to the proper balance of nature are recognized as key factors in the ecosystem. Their interdependence with prey species in our environment is accepted, protected and even encouraged. Even preservationists have come to realize that certain prey species experience population explosions—with all their attendant disasters of starvation and disease—when they are allowed to expand without the check imposed by traditional predators in their home range.

A great many animal protectionists are not only sincere, but sensible people. They recognize the problems of over-population and nature's role in taking care of the situation. Many animal lovers have come to accept—even venerate—the role of the animal predator. Unfortunately, few protection-oriented animal enthusiasts can accept the fact that in many cases man is the only predator available to accomplish the job that must be done to ensure the sound survival of certain prey species adjacent to settled areas.

Man—either in urban or agricultural communities—is unprepared to accept certain of the large predators in close proximity to either his family or his livestock. Nothing any of us—hunter or protectionist—can say will convince the suburban and exurban towns of New Jersey that the Somerset County deer herd needs a good pack of timber wolves or an occasional family of eastern panthers to keep it in healthy balance. Understandable and completely justified. Similarly, but less justifiably, no one is going to convince a Montana sheepman or cattleman that grizzlies are not the devil's own creatures.

So there you are. What do you do about the fantastic overpopulation of deer in many areas of the continental United States? Who is going to harvest the surplus elk herd in the Yellowstone Park? Man in his traditional role of the hunter is the obvious, logical and only acceptable solution, but he is violently rejected—and the animals involved are often condemned to biological disaster—by the very people who fiercely declare their unswerving dedication to those same four-footed creatures of the forest.

Strangely, there are those among the anti-hunting faction who have actually endorsed the elimination of animal herds rather than allowing them to be hunted. I have actually heard this proposition seriously advanced by so-called well-meaning and sensible people. The fact is granted that animals will breed and increase beyond their food supply; that further they cannot be trimmed back except by human control; and that, lastly, this is intolerable from an ethical standpoint because it turns man into a killer who kills for pleasure and this must be prevented at all cost—in this case, the lives of the very animals involved! In the last analysis then, the animals don't really count, and in that I think we have at least a hint of the key to the antihunting phenomena.

This element in the antihunting movement advances the following argument for their position: There are animals—both wild and domestic—that must and, indeed, should be harvested for the good of mankind. These antihunters accept this because it is an economic and biological necessity. Certain animals are taken for food and other products; others are eliminated for less palatable, but equally justified, reasons—they are dangerous or simply obnoxious to man, or they compete with man for land and water, probably the most heinous crime of all. Ergo, wild animals must go, but they must be dispatched as domestic animals are slaughtered—dispassionately, impersonally and, hopefully, by surrogate killers who will do the dirty deed quickly, efficiently, and discreetly out of everyone's view. In order to quell any twinges of conscience and salve any lingering doubts, the killing must not give pleasure to anyone—no sport or satisfaction in an animal taken in fair chase. There must be no chance of the animal surviving or the whole program would be pointless. After all, the idea is to save man from himself and his base hunter's nature. There is only one way to do that—remove the cause and chance of temptation, the animals themselves.

As you can see, this particular odd lot of antihunters could really not care less about animals; they are concerned with salvation as they see it, and heaven help the poor benighted heathen—in this case, you and me—who don't agree to be saved. The key to their position is simply this: they cannot accept the facts of life and death, that we men are animals as any other and as we now live, so shall we one day die as all life must. Albert Schweitzer developed the "reverence for life" theory, the cornerstone of this philosophy, and it simply holds that all life is sacred and must be preserved at all costs. (Schweitzer selectively chose which life he thought was sacred around the pea patches of his African medical compound.) Modern advocates of "reverence for life" have become even more discriminating in their implementation of Schweitzer's philosophy and, by and large, take a Puritan's view that the only killing to be stopped is that involved with sports hunting. God deliver us all from well-meaning, divinely inspired crusaders. Perhaps they simply are incapable of understanding what again Theodore Roosevelt knew and expressed so well:

> In hunting, the finding and killing of the game is after all but a part of the whole. The free, self-reliant, adventurous life, with its rugged and stalwart democracy; the wild surroundings, the grand beauty of the scenery, the chance to study the ways and habits of the woodland creatures—all these unite to give to the career of the wilderness hunter its peculiar charm. The chase is among the best of all national pastimes; it cultivates that vigorous manliness for the lack of which in a nation, as in an individual, the possession of no other qualities can possibly atone.

President Roosevelt had no problem assuming the dual roles of "the mighty hunter" and America's father of conservation. With an almost uncanny foresight, his words of the turn of the century have as much meaning now as they did then:

> In order to preserve the wildlife of the wilderness at all, some middle ground must be found between brutal and senseless slaughter and the unhealthy sentimentalism which would just as surely defeat its own end by bringing about the eventual total extinction of the game. It is impossible to preserve the larger wild animals in regions thoroughly fit for agriculture; and it is perhaps too much to hope that the larger carnivores can be preserved for merely aesthetic reasons. But throughout our country there are large regions entirely unsuited for agriculture, where if people only have foresight, they can, through the power of the state, keep the game in perpetuity.

I am sure it must seem singularly strange to many non-hunters—and, of course, to antihunters—that a group of men and women who have obviously spent a great deal of time and effort pursuing and often killing wild animals should be so concerned with their continued well-being.

Perhaps, as Oscar Wilde once said, "Each man kills the thing he loves," but I would prefer to think that our dedication both as individuals and collectively runs a much deeper course than that rather epigrammatic quotation might indicate.

While there is scarcely time to delve further into the philosophical and pragmatic justifications of sport hunting, let it suffice to say that the record speaks for itself on the question of who has largely paid the bills for conservation through the years. As an example, there would be no wildlife management—or, indeed, wildlife populations of any size—in the United States if the hunter had not provided the economic wherewithal in the form of licenses, fees and special taxes on arms and ammunition to both the federal government and the various state agencies concerned with wildlife. There was a time not too distant when conservationists and their societies—and their concern for wildlife—were regarded by the great mass of people as some sort of freaks who ran around in tennis shoes carrying signs and generally making nuisances of themselves. Now, with the newly awakened interest in ecology and the total environment, the sportsman is receiving a much-needed and welcomed assist from a broad spectrum of the body politic—hopefully, on a lasting basis and not only as a sometime fad to be abandoned when other, more alluring, siren songs sound in the future.

The time, treasure and talent offered up—freely and willingly—over the past half-century by organizations like Ducks Unlimited, the Izaak Walton League, the Camp Fire Club, the Boone & Crockett Club, the National Wildlife Federation and countless state and local organizations cannot be measured in material terms alone.

The vast game herds that have been brought back from near extinction in North America bring pleasure to all Americans, hunter or not, and who can say how much money or time went into the effort and what it is worth in dollars and cents? We, as hunters, bear a responsibility beyond the ordinary citizen. Since we have taken the privilege of hunting individual wild animals, we must accept the custodianship of their overall well-being as various species. We must never take an animal without reason—and good reason—or we have committed the worst sin of all, for to kill without meaning degrades an animal and implies that its life meant nothing. In the last analysis, we might all keep in mind as we venture forth on our various hunts, large and small, through the world:

> *A ravaged hillside is an affront to all men's eyes.*
> *A polluted stream knows no boundaries and flows by*
> *   everyman's village.*
> *A poisoned atmosphere is breathed into the lungs of*
> *   all men, black or white, rich or poor, young or old.*
> *And lastly, a slaughtered game population is a crime*
> *   against all living creatures.*

Perhaps one day there will no longer be hunting as we know it now and animals will be seen only in somewhat artificial circumstances in game reserves and zoos. I hope not, but if it be so, let those who are left to enjoy this sequestered wildlife remember those who did so much to guarantee its survival. And if we hunters leave any epitaph let it be that future generations will say: They gave more than they took.

That will be our moment of truth.